Haydn Ri[illegible]

Junior En[illegible]

Ginn and Company Ltd

Acknowledgements

Grateful acknowledgement is made to the following for permission to use copyright material:

page 12 **Raman meets the rocking-horse**
The Rocking-Horse by Rosemary Manning. By kind permission of Hamish Hamilton Ltd.

18 **Some useful finds**
The Bicycle Wheel by Ruth Ainsworth. By kind permission of Hamish Hamilton Ltd.

78 **The end of the race**
The Truce of the Games by Rosemary Sutcliff. By kind permission of Murray Pollinger Ltd.

84 **A bear cub's adventure**
Baby Mishook by Leon Golschmann. By kind permission of The Bodley Head.

Designed by Michael Soderberg with Alan Miller
Illustrated by Barry Rowe, Martin White and Beverly Curl

Revised edition 1981
Twenty-sixth impression 1996 049611
ISBN 0 602 22549 3 (without answers)
ISBN 0 602 22617 1 (with answers)
Published by Ginn and Company
Prebendal House, Parson's Fee,
Aylesbury, Bucks HP20 2QY
Filmset by Filmtype Services Limited, Scarborough
Printed in Great Britain at the University Press, Cambridge

Preface

The main aim of Haydn Richards Junior English is to enable the pupil to work alone, as far as is possible. For this reason complete lists of the words needed to answer the various exercises are given. Being thus provided with the necessary tools the pupil should experience little difficulty in doing the work.

The course provides ample and varied practice in all the English topics usually taught in the Junior School. Such simple grammatical terms as are essential to the understanding of the language are introduced at appropriate stages, together with simple definitions, lucid explanations and easy examples.

The meaning of every proverb and idiom dealt with is given, so that these may be used correctly in both writing and conversation.

A noteworthy feature of each book in the series is the detailed alphabetical Contents facilitating reference to any particular topic by the teacher and the older pupils.

In addition to teaching and testing such topics as Parts of Speech, Opposites, Synonyms, Homophones, Punctuation, Direct and Indirect Speech, Sentence Linkage and Structure, etc., the course includes verbal intelligence exercises designed to stimulate clear thinking, so that by the end of the fourth year the pupil who has worked steadily through the course is well equipped for any entrance examination.

H.R.

Contents

Nouns naming words

The dog followed the boy.
dog is the **name** of an animal.
boy is the **name** of a person.

A noun is the name of a person or thing.

A Find the nouns in these sentences. Write them in your book.

1 The window was broken.
2 I lost my knife.
3 This pencil is too short.
4 The cake was stale.
5 The bird flew away.
6 The sea beat against the rocks.
7 The dog barked at the postman.
8 Summer is the warmest season.
9 The plane landed safely.
10 Only one apple was left on the dish.

B Name three things you might find in—

1 a toy shop
2 a farmyard
3 a kitchen
4 a railway station
5 a car
6 a hospital
7 a cinema
8 a church

Use your dictionary.

Verbs doing words

The butcher cut the meat and weighed it.

The words **cut** and **weighed** tell what the butcher **did** to the meat.

These are **doing** words, or **action** words.

A verb is a word which shows action.

A Find the verbs in these sentences. Write them in your book.

1 The little girl cried.

2 We cut a lot of wood for the fire.

3 Please pass me the jam.

4 Roy knocked at the door of the office.

5 Two robins hopped on to the window-ledge.

6 Pam put her toys away and went to bed.

7 After school John cycles to the park and plays cricket.

8 The clown smiled when we waved to him.

9 Henry told his mother that he liked cream cakes.

10 Carol ate four sweets and gave the rest away.

B Name three actions which might be done by each of these persons.

Example a baby cry, play, suck

1 a doctor

2 a footballer

3 your teacher

4 a gardener

5 a cricketer

6 a policeman

7 a pupil in your class

8 a farmer

Vowels

Instead of **a** always write **an** before words beginning with

a e i o u

These letters are called **vowels**.

acorn
anchor
apple
apron
arch
arm
arrow
axe
easel
eel
egg
envelope
eye
island
oar
orange
orchard

A Write the names of these things, putting **an** before each.
You will find them in the list on the left.

B Write **a** or **an** before each of these words.

1	____ book	9	____ chair
2	____ ant	10	____ organ
3	____ apple	11	____ ox
4	____ rock	12	____ elf
5	____ oval	13	____ sweet
6	____ egg	14	____ hat
7	____ flag	15	____ imp
8	____ inn	16	____ shoe

C Write **a** or **an** to finish the sentences.

1 Pauline ate ____ apple and ____ banana.

2 Mother gave ____ order for a new piano.

3 We came to ____ lake with ____ island in the middle.

4 Linda is spending ____ holiday with ____ aunt in London.

5 ____ east wind is colder than ____ west wind.

Verbs adding -ed and -ing

A Write **-ing** after each word.

1	look	4	teach	7	read
2	walk	5	pay	8	camp
3	push	6	go	9	wear

B Write **-ed** after each word.

1	stay	4	rush	7	fill
2	post	5	touch	8	end
3	work	6	help	9	turn

C Write **-ing** after each word.
Drop the **e** at the end.
Example serve serving

1	blaze	4	love	7	raise
2	dance	5	share	8	hope
3	dare	6	waste		

D Write **-ed** after each word.
Drop the **e** at the end.
Example place placed

1	taste	4	hate	7	snore
2	live	5	chase	8	close
3	rattle	6	blame		

E Write the missing words by adding **-ing** or **-ed** to the verbs in bold type.

1 We saw a small dog ____ a cat. **chase**

2 The fire ____ when a log was put on it. **blaze**

3 The old man was ____ most of the night. **snore**

4 Nobody ____ to answer the door. **dare**

5 Paul sat on the rug ____ the cat. **stroke**

6 We got there just as the shop was ____ . **close**

Adjectives describing words

The queen of the fairies had a golden wand.

The word **golden** tells us **what kind** of **wand** it was.

Because it describes the noun **wand**, we call it an **adjective**.

An adjective is a word which describes a noun.

A Pick out and write the adjectives in these sentences.

1 A big lorry was parked outside the school.

2 The rough sea upset the boys.

3 Claire wore a new dress at the party.

4 The baby was playing with a huge teddy bear.

5 The torch gave a brilliant light.

6 The captain of the ship had a wooden leg.

7 It was easy to wade through the shallow river.

8 We helped the blind man across the road.

9 It was such a busy street.

10 At the circus we saw a clever monkey riding a bicycle.

B Choose an adjective from the list on the left to fill each of the spaces below.

loud	sharp
tidy	white
heavy	savage
juicy	leather
deep	beautiful

1 a ____ doll

2 a ____ knife

3 a ____ noise

4 a ____ dog

5 a ____ shower

6 a ____ pear

7 a ____ belt

8 a ____ room

9 a ____ sheet

10 a ____ cut

Cinderella

Cinderella ran to the garden and brought her godmother the finest pumpkin she could find, wondering how this would help her to go to the ball.

The godmother scooped out the inside of the pumpkin, leaving nothing but the rind. Then she touched it with her magic wand, and the pumpkin was changed in a moment into a fine coach, all shining with gold.

After that she went to look into the mouse-trap, where she found six mice, all alive. She told Cinderella to lift the trap-door up a little, and as each mouse came out she gave it a tap with her wand. At once it was changed into a beautiful horse. This made a very fine team of six horses, all dappled grey in colour.

Tales from Perrault

1 What did the godmother do with the pumpkin?
2 With what did she touch the pumpkin?
3 What happened when she did this?
4 What did the godmother find in the mouse-trap?
5 What did she tell Cinderella to do?
6 What did the godmother do as each mouse came out?
7 What happened to each mouse?
8 What was the colour of each horse?

Questions

Every question must have a question mark(?) at the end.

Examples
Why were you so late?
Where have you been?

why
have
who
when
how
did
what
which
whose
where

Use the words in the list on the left to fill the spaces in the questions below.

Remember to put a question mark (?) at the end of each question.

A

1 ____ you enjoy the tea

2 ____ are you today

3 ____ told you about the party

4 ____ were you absent yesterday

5 ____ did you have for dinner

6 ____ are you coming to see me

7 ____ of these books do you like best

8 ____ has mother put the sweets

9 ____ cap is this

10 ____ you been to London

B Write five sentences of your own, each beginning with one of the words from the list above.

The weather

When the weather is wet,
We must not fret.
When the weather is cold,
We must not scold.
When the weather is warm
We must not storm,
But be thankful together
Whatever the weather.

A The words in the list on the left are used to describe weather. Write these sentences in your book, filling each space with a word from the list.

breezy
stormy
foggy
sunny
rainy
windy
misty
icy
showery
thundery

1 When the wind is blowing hard it is ____ .
2 When the sun is shining it is ____ .
3 When there is a fog it is ____ .
4 When there is a mist it is ____ .
5 When the rain pours it is a ____ day.
6 When there is a storm it is ____ .
7 When there is a breeze it is ____ .
8 When there is thunder it is ____ .
9 When there are showers the weather is ____ .
10 When the wind is as cold as ice it is ____ .

B Write two or three sentences about any two of these.

1 a sunny morning
2 a cold afternoon
3 a wet afternoon
4 a windy day
5 a stormy sea
6 a foggy night

showeryfoggy*icy*sunny***windy***

Using the right word

is
The wind **is** cold.

his
Tom lost **his** book.

as
You are **as** tall **as** Janet.

has
Anne **has** a new coat.

did
He **did** his work well.

done
He has **done** his work well.
helping word **has**

is
This apple **is** sour.
one

are
These apples **are** sour.
more than one

was
The boy **was** happy.
one

were
The boys **were** happy.
more than one

saw
We **saw** the Tower of London.

seen
We have **seen** the Tower of London.
helping word **have**

A Choose the right word from the pair above to fill each space.

1 **is** **his**
He can't run because ____ leg ____ stiff.

2 **was** **were**
The boy ____ afraid of the bull.

3 **was** **were**
Several cows ____ grazing in the field.

4 **as** **has**
She cannot come ____ she ____ too much work to do.

5 **is** **his**
Roger ____ going to visit ____ grandmother.

6 **as** **has**
Joy ____ a lump ____ big ____ an egg on her forehead.

B Write the word which will fill each gap.

1 **saw** **seen**
Three people ____ the accident.

2 **did** **done**
Sarah ____ her best to tidy the garage.

3 **is** **are**
The book ____ kept on the shelf.

4 **did** **done**
Philip rested when he had ____ his work.

5 **saw** **seen**
It is the biggest trout I have ____ .

6 **is** **are**
The books ____ kept on the shelf.

Words with more than one meaning

Some words have more than one meaning.

Examples
The brown **bear** climbed the tree.
Sandra could hardly **bear** the pain.

bark	light
blow	match
chest	ring
fair	shed
kind	watch

Use the words in the list on the left to fill the spaces in the sentences. The same word must be used for each pair of sentences.

1. The lawn mower is kept in the garden ____ .
   Many trees ____ their leaves in the autumn.
2. The ____ woman put £1 in the collecting box.
   This is a different ____ of toffee.
3. It is time to ____ the school bell.
   The wedding ____ was made of solid gold.
4. The oak tree has a rough ____ .
   The dog began to ____ when the children teased him
5. Much damage is done when high winds ____ .
   A ____ on the head knocked the boxer out.
6. Shirley has very ____ hair.
   There were many amusements at the ____ .
7. My new ____ keeps very good time.
   We did not ____ television last night.
8. The parcel was as ____ as a feather.
   In winter we ____ the fire every day.
9. There was a big crowd at the football ____ .
   Father struck a ____ and lit his pipe.
10. James has a cold on his ____ .
    The tools are kept in a big wooden ____ .

Using capital letters

Capital letters are used:

to begin a sentence	**A**lways start a sentence with a capital letter.
to begin every line of poetry	**T**he world is so full of a number of things **I**'m sure we should all be as happy as kings.
for the names of people and pets	**G**eorge, **J**ennifer, **F**luffy, **P**ongo Also for **M**r., **M**rs., **D**r.
for the names of places, rivers, mountains and so on	**B**ristol, **T**hames, **S**nowdon, **A**tlantic
for addresses	29 **S**outh **R**oad, **B**arnsdale, **BA**12 3**QT**.
for the names of the days of the week	**M**onday, **W**ednesday, **S**aturday
for the word I	**I** did my best but **I** failed.

Copy these sentences, using capital letters where they are needed.

1 henry chaplin lives in hastings.

2 the national gallery has some beautiful paintings.

3 david and i are going to london for a day.

4 we hope to go next friday.

5 the highest mountain in wales is snowdon.

6 canterbury is in kent.

7 a new shop has opened in bond street.

8 up into the cherry tree
who should go but little me?

9 colin has a pet dog named pepper.

10 we paid a visit to mr. and mrs. reeve.

Raman meets the rocking-horse

Raman asked his mother after school if he could go home and play with Jock. She said "Yes", and she would come and fetch him at half-past five. She wore a long, flowing sari, and Jock thought she was very beautiful. "She's an Indian princess," he thought. "I'll ride to her rescue if she's in danger."

When they reached Jock's house, Jock took Raman into the basement room, and went up to the horse and patted his neck.

"What's he called?" asked Raman, gazing at the horse with admiration.

"I don't know yet," answered Jock and added quickly: "At least I do, but his name's a secret. He only allows *me* to call him by it."

This was not quite true, as Jock hadn't yet invented a name for him, but he knew that he would sometime.

"He's wonderful," breathed Raman. "Can I have a ride?"

"Well, he doesn't like strangers much," answered Jock. "I'll ride him first so that he can look at you and get used to you."

The Rocking-Horse Rosemary Manning

At what time of day did Raman go to play with Jock?
From which country do you think Raman's mother came?
What is the name of the long robe worn by women of that country?
Why did Jock think of Raman's mother as a princess?
In what part of the house was the rocking-horse kept?
What reason did Jock give Raman for not telling him the horse's name?
What was Jock's real reason for not telling him?
What reason did Jock give Raman for having the first ride himself?

Here and hear/There and their

here
means **in this place**.

I left the bag **here** five minutes ago.

hear
You **hear** with your ears.

We could **hear** the thrushes singing.

A Write **here** or **hear** in each space.

1 Will you stay ____ till I come back?

2 Ann did not ____ her mother calling her.

3 We could ____ someone snoring in the next room.

4 ____ is the ball you were looking for.

5 Would you like to live ____ ?

6 Deaf people cannot ____ .

there
means **in that place**.

He lives over **there**.

their
means **belonging to them**.

The boys played with **their** football.

B Write **there** or **their** in each space.

1 The children gave ____ dog a bath.

2 I waited ____ for nearly an hour.

3 ____ are a hundred pence in a pound.

4 Is ____ room for me to sit down?

5 The two boys went to the show with ____ cousin.

6 I saw patches of clover here and ____ on the lawn.

Plurals

Singular means **one**.

Plural means **more than one**.

Singular	**Plural**
boy	boys
glass	glasses
daisy	daisies
leaf	leaves

A Add **-s** to each word to form the plural.

1 bird
2 cook
3 head
4 farmer
5 tree
6 chair
7 river
8 coat

B Add **-es** to each word to form the plural.

1 bush
2 bunch
3 coach
4 brush
5 box
6 dish
7 church
8 match

C Change **y** to **i** and add **-es**.

1 fly
2 pony
3 baby
4 berry
5 story
6 lady
7 gipsy
8 penny

D Change **f** to **v** and add **-es**.

1 elf
2 shelf
3 loaf
4 half
5 calf
6 leaf
7 wolf
8 sheaf

E Copy these sentences, making each noun in bold type plural.

Example 1 They fed the calves on milk.

1 They fed the **calf** on milk.

2 The **butcher** sharpened the **knife**.

3 The **baker** put the burnt **loaf** on the **shelf**.

4 The **gardener** trimmed the **bush**.

5 The **gipsy** fed the **pony**.

6 The **leaf** fell from the **tree**.

7 The **fly** buzzed round the **baby**.

8 The **sweep** put the **brush** in the **box**.

Verbs adding -ed and -ing

When we add **-ed** or **-ing** to each of the words in this list we double the last letter.

nod
nodded
nodding

hum
hummed
humming

drop
dropped
dropping

grin
grinned
grinning

A Add **-ing** to each word, first doubling the last letter.

1	peg	6	skim
2	chat	7	drop
3	rob	8	skid
4	stab	9	drag
5	hum	10	slip

B Add **-ed** to each word, first doubling the last letter.

1	snap	6	dip
2	grin	7	trim
3	lap	8	grab
4	rub	9	slam
5	nod	10	drip

C Fill each space with the right verb.

1 Water was ____ from a hole in the can.

2 The car ____ on the wet road and crashed.

3 Joy ____ a merry tune as she went along.

4 Mother ____ the wet clothes on the line.

5 The rude boy ____ the door as he went out.

6 Alan ____ on a banana skin and hurt his leg.

7 The gardener was busy ____ the hedge.

8 A lovely white kitten was ____ a saucer of milk.

Joining sentences using so

You have learnt how to join sentences using the words **and** or **but** as links.

two sentences	Father poked the fire. He put coal on it.
one sentence	Father poked the fire **and** put coal on it.
two sentences	We looked for the book. We failed to find it.
one sentence	We looked for the book **but** failed to find it.

The word **so** is also used as a link.

two sentences	It started to rain. We went home.
one sentence	It started to rain **so** we went home.

Join each pair of sentences using the word **so**.

1 It was a fine day.
We went down to the beach.

2 Paul had lost his bus fare.
He had to walk home.

3 The old man was tired.
He sat down to rest.

4 The children had mumps.
They could not go to school.

5 Bill had no money.
He could not buy an ice cream.

6 Charles felt hot.
He took his coat off.

7 The weather was wet.
We wore our boots.

8 The soil in the garden was very wet.
The gardener could not dig it.

Forming nouns

Some nouns are formed by adding **-ness** to words.

sad	sadness
slow	slowness
deaf	deafness
stout	stoutness

When **-ness** is added to words ending with **y**, the **y** is changed to **i**.

steady	steadiness
shabby	shabbiness
sleepy	sleepiness

A Add **-ness** to these words.

1	glad	6	greedy	11	sore
2	stale	7	lame	12	sad
3	quick	8	blind	13	giddy
4	tired	9	rough	14	wicked
5	loud	10	fresh	15	good

B Fill each space with the noun formed from the word in bold type.

1 Jennie thanked her teacher for her ____ . **kind**

2 The wolves started to howl as ____ fell. **dark**

3 Winter often brings much ____ . **ill**

4 It is ____ to speed on busy roads. **mad**

5 The wood was two centimetres in ____ . **thick**

6 The old man was suffering from ____ . **giddy**

7 We were surprised at the ____ of the performing lions. **tame**

8 The man's ____ was caused by an explosion. **deaf**

9 Mrs. Platt scolded Bobby for his ____ . **lazy**

10 Gerald was dazzled by the ____ of the sun. **bright**

Some useful finds

Just then the rubbish dump came into sight, and they started to run towards it. It was a flattish hill of ashes and cinders, mixed with old tyres and broken furniture.

James and Jenny began to climb over this hill of rubbish, exclaiming every time they found a treasure. Penny followed, not liking the dust that rose under her feet, and the crunch of the cinders, but was as pleased as the others when she found a big bundle of paper with one side plain.

"Drawing paper!" she called out. "Scribbling paper! Sheets and sheets and sheets. We can make it pretty, and paper the whole of the dolls' house. We can play schools, too."

"A chain" said James, clanking it joyfully. "A strong, useful chain. We can play at prisons and I'll chain you up."

The Bicycle Wheel Ruth Ainsworth

1 What four things did the rubbish dump consist of?
2 Explain what is meant by the word "treasure" in this passage.
3 What did James and Jenny do every time they found a treasure?
4 What two things did Penny not like about the dump?
5 What made Penny pleased when she looked through the dump?
6 What three things did Penny want to do with the paper?
7 What did James do when he found the chain?
8 How did James describe the chain?
9 What did he suggest they did with it?
10 How do you think the children felt as they climbed over the dump?

Adjectives describing words

Adjectives can be formed by adding **-y** to some words.

rust	rusty
greed	greedy
wealth	wealthy
storm	stormy

When **-y** is added to some words the last letter of the word is doubled.

sun	sunny
fog	foggy
skin	skinny
fur	furry
bag	baggy

When **-y** is added to a word ending with **e** this letter is dropped.

noise	noisy
smoke	smoky
ease	easy
shade	shady
stone	stony

A What are the missing words?

1 Hands covered with dirt ____ hands
2 A day of strong winds a ____ day
3 A mountain with many rocks a ____ mountain
4 A beach covered with sand a ____ beach
5 A table covered with dust a ____ table
6 A chest covered with hair a ____ chest
7 Hair which has curls ____ hair
8 Food which has a lot of salt ____ food
9 A sky with many clouds a ____ sky
10 A girl who has lots of luck a ____ girl

B What are the missing adjectives?

1 a ____ day **sun**
2 an ____ chair **ease**
3 a ____ hand **skin**
4 a ____ animal **fur**
5 a ____ chimney **smoke**
6 a ____ class **noise**
7 ____ trousers **bag**
8 a ____ tree **shade**
9 a ____ path **stone**
10 a ____ night **fog**

Verbs adding -es and -ed

When **-es** or **-ed** is added to a verb ending with **y**, this letter is first changed to **i**.

I **try** hard.

He **tries** hard.

She **tried** hard.

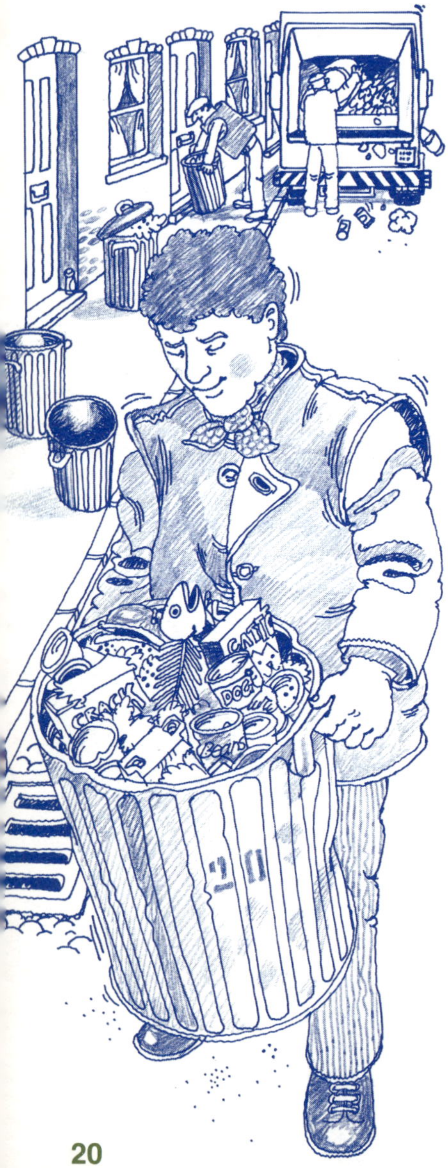

A Copy and fill in the missing letters.

1	try	. . . es	6	dirty	. . . . . es
2	cry	. . . ed	7	copy	. . . . ed
3	dry	. . . ed	8	empty	. . . . . es
4	fry	. . . es	9	hurry	. . . . . ed
5	spy	. . . ed	10	carry	. . . . . es

B Finish each sentence by using the right form of the verb in bold type, adding **-es** or **-ed** as needed.

1 Paul . . . . . bacon and eggs for my breakfast this morning. **fry**

2 Every day Ann . . . . . . sums from Angela. **copy**

3 She . . . . . because she had cut her knee. **cry**

4 Although we . . . . to the station we missed the train. **hurry**

5 Again and again the little spider . . . . . to climb up the thread. **try**

6 David . . . . his books to school in a satchel. **carry**

7 Every time she washes her hands she . . . . . them well. **dry**

8 Yesterday the dustmen . . . . all the bins in our street. **empty**

9 I . . . . . a rook up on the church tower. **spy**

10 Mark . . . . his hands so he went to wash them. **dirty**

Same sound — different meaning

Some words have the same sound as other words, but they are different in spelling and meaning.

Look at these four pairs of words.

bare	A **bare** tree has no leaves.
bear	The polar **bear** is a very big animal.
dear	The dress was too **dear** so she did not buy it. Jane is a very **dear** friend of mine.
deer	A **deer** is a graceful animal.
fair	**Fair** hair is light in colour. We had fun at the **fair**.
fare	The bus conductor asked me for my **fare**.
heel	The back part of your foot is called the **heel**.
heal	To **heal** a person means to make him well.

dear
dear
de—r
deer
deer

Choose the correct word from the pair above to complete each sentence.

1 **fair** **fare**
The bus ____ to school is twenty pence.

2 **heel** **heal**
The cut on your finger will soon ____ .

3 **bear** **bare**
The big brown ____ sat up and begged.

4 **heel** **heal**
The ____ of the woman's shoe came right off.

5 **fair** **fare**
Peter won a coconut at the ____ .

6 **bear** **bare**
Many trees are ____ in winter.

7 **dear** **deer**
We saw ten ____ in the park.

Full stops/Commas

A **full stop** is put at the end of every telling sentence.

Example
I hung my coat on the coat-hanger.

A **question mark** is put at the end of every question.

Example
Did you hang your coat on the coat-hanger?

A Copy each sentence. Put a full stop or a question mark at the end of each

1 The bushy tail of a fox is called a brush
2 A camel can go for days without water
3 Have you visited the Tower of London
4 The Nile is a long river in Africa
5 Will you call for me in the morning
6 Our school starts at nine o'clock
7 Did you post the letter I gave you
8 Beavers can gnaw through big trees

When the names of three or more things come together, we separate them by using **commas**. (,)

Example
For tea we had cakes**,** jelly**,** fruit and trifle.

Notice that there is no comma between the last two things. The word **and** separates them.

B Copy these sentences. Put in the commas.

1 Robert Andrew Michael and Peter were ill.
2 The fishmonger had hake plaice herrings mackerel and cod.
3 London York Birmingham and Exeter are all cities.
4 The colours of the rainbow are red orange yellow green blue indigo and violet.
5 At the zoo we saw lions tigers elephants camels and monkeys.

Similars

A **wealthy** man
A **rich** man

The words **wealthy** and **rich** have much the same meaning.

Learn the list of similars before answering the questions.

collect	gather
difficult	hard
pile	heap
commence	begin
hasten	hurry
peril	danger
weeping	crying
drowsy	sleepy
naked	bare
plucky	brave

A Write a simpler word in place of each word in bold type.

1 The concert will **commence** at 7 o'clock.

2 Jill found the sum very **difficult**.

3 The ship was in great **peril**.

4 A **pile** of stones lay outside the school.

5 The **plucky** sailor saved the boy's life.

6 At the funeral several women were **weeping**.

7 Sitting near a big fire makes one **drowsy**.

8 The sun shone on the swimmer's **naked** back.

B In each group below select the word which is similar in meaning to the word in bold type.

1 **drowsy**
lively
quick
active
sleepy

2 **hasten**
fix
hurry
work
play

3 **collect**
give
spend
gather
climb

4 **difficult**
clever
easy
hard
simple

5 **peril**
danger
length
safety
depth

6 **plucky**
silly
brave
short
noisy

7 **assist**
help
coax
hinder
wait

8 **halt**
hurry
linger
run
stop

Tom and the otters

As Tom was sitting on a water-lily leaf watching the gnats dance, he heard the strangest noise up the stream. He looked up the water, and there he saw a great ball rolling over and over down the stream, seeming one moment of soft brown fur, and the next of shining glass.

And when he came near, the ball turned out to be four or five beautiful creatures, many times larger than Tom, who were swimming about, and rolling and diving and twisting in the most charming fashion. Tom did not know that they were otters at play.

But when the biggest of them saw Tom, she darted out from the rest, and cried in the water-language sharply enough, "Quick, children, here is something to eat!" and came at poor Tom showing a wicked pair of eyes and a set of sharp teeth. But Tom slipped in between the water-lily roots as fast as he could, and then turned round and made faces at her.

The Water Babies Charles Kingsley

1 Where was Tom sitting when this happened?
2 What was he watching?
3 What did he hear up the stream?
4 What did Tom see rolling over and over down the stream?
5 Name two things that it looked like.
6 What did the beautiful creatures turn out to be?
7 Name four things which these creatures were doing.
8 How did Tom escape from them?

Fun with words

In each column below there are two pairs of words and one odd word.

You have to find the word which will make up the third pair.

Look at the first pair of words in **A**: **ear** **hear**

The second word is made by adding the letter **h** to the beginning of the first word.

Look at the second pair: **at** **hat**

The second word is again formed by writing **h** before the first word.

To find the missing word write **h** before the odd word.

Example **arm** **harm**

A Now find the other missing words. In every column a different letter must be added.

1 ear hear
at hat
arm ____

2 all ball
eat beat
oil ____

3 ark park
ink pink
lay ____

4 ill mill
ask mask
other ____

5 old gold
lad glad
race ____

B In each line below the same letter ends the first word and begins the second. Write the ten pairs of words.

Example sat tea

1	sa .	. ea
2	be .	. og
3	sh .	. gg
4	bi .	. un
5	wa .	. ly
6	pos .	. rap
7	fil .	. ift
8	goo .	. oor
9	hea .	. ich
10	hel .	. lay

Showing ownership

I like Simon's new puppy.

The **'s** in Simon's shows that the puppy **belongs** to Simon. It is **his**. He **owns** it.

A Copy these in your book, putting in the **'** before the **s**.

1 the robin s breast
2 the sailor s cap
3 the horse s mane
4 the rabbit s tail
5 the old man s beard
6 the grocer s apron
7 the gipsy s caravan
8 the sheep s wool
9 the Queen s crown
10 the dog s collar

the kite which belongs to Paul (*long way*)

Paul's kite (*short way*)

B Write these the short way.

1 the book belonging to Mary
2 the bat which belongs to Peter
3 the ribbon belonging to Ann
4 the watch which belongs to Father
5 the ring which belongs to Mother

the wool of the sheep (*long way*)

the sheep's wool (*short way*)

C Write these the short way.

1 the fur of the cat
2 the den of the lion
3 the beak of the blackbird
4 the ears of the donkey
5 the horns of the cow

Pictures and sentences

Look at the first picture. Find the sentence which matches it. Write it in your book. Do the same with the other pictures and sentences.

1	2	3	4
5	6	7	8

The dog is chasing the cat.

There were two cows grazing in the meadow.

The man is taking his dog for a walk.

The woman is riding a horse.

The farmer is driving the tractor.

The horse is in the stable.

The hens are pecking food in the yard.

The woman is carrying apples in her basket.

Alphabetical order

Look at the alphabet.

abcd
efgh
ijklm
nopq
rstuv
wxyz

A

1 Write the third letter of the alphabet.

2 Which letter is last but one?

3 Which letter comes between **j** and **l**?

4 What are the missing letters?
g h . j k . m n o . q

B Write each group of words in **a-b-c** or alphabetical order. Look at the first letter of each word.

1 head, train, before, food, also

2 look, ready, winter, another, small

3 green, water, cross, idea, pull

4 paint, teach, little, heart, alone

5 please, answer, mountain, young, under

C In each group below all the words are in alphabetical order except one. Write the odd word in each group.

Example Group 1 bicycle

1 night, orange, pretty, queen, bicycle

2 army, bread, colour, letter, doctor

3 early, dress, figure, garden, house

4 kitchen, length, window, mouse, north

5 beauty, heavy, ground, middle, season

Short forms

You have learnt how to join two words, one of which is **not**.

is not	isn't
was not	wasn't
does not	doesn't
has not	hasn't

Notice that the **'** stands for the **o** which is left out.

We can also join **is** to another word in this way.

he is	he's
she is	she's
it is	it's
who is	who's
that is	that's
what is	what's
where is	where's
there is	there's

Remember that the **'** stands for the **i** which is left out.

Write these sentences, joining the two words in bold type in each.

1 Brian says **he is** too busy to play.

2 I think **that is** a lovely dress.

3 Carol is tall, and **she is** pretty, too.

4 Thank goodness **it is** a fine day.

5 We can't work when **there is** a noise in the room.

6 I can guess **what is** in the box.

7 I wonder **who is** going to the party tonight.

8 **It is** not raining now.

9 Roger **does not** like going to town.

10 The pears **are not** quite ripe.

Rhymes

Read this poem, then answer the questions.

A spring song

See the yellow catkins cover
All the slender willows over;
And on mossy banks so green
Star-like primroses are seen;
And their clustering leaves below,
White and purple violets grow.

Hark! the little lambs are bleating,
And the cawing rooks are meeting
In the elms – a noisy crowd;
And all the birds are singing loud,
There, the first white butterfly
In the sun goes flitting by.

Mary Howitt

1 Write the word which rhymes with **meeting**.

2 Which word rhymes with **seen**?

3 **Grow** rhymes with **below**. Write three other words which rhyme with these two.

4 Give the word which rhymes with **over**.

5 Which two words in the poem rhyme with **proud**?

6 Write the word which rhymes with the name of an insect in the poem.

7 Which two words end with the same sound as **greeting**?

8 Write three words beginning with **c**, **d** and **f** which rhyme with **by**.

Noises of animals

A Write the noise words.

1 sheep ____
2 pigs ____
3 dogs ____
4 cows ____
5 donkeys ____
6 cockerels ____
7 hens ____
8 cats ____

B Fill each space with the name of the creature or the name of the noise it makes.

1 The dog was ____ at a gipsy.

2 We heard the cows ____ in the meadow.

3 The loud braying of a ____ frightened the children.

4 The cat was ____ because she had hurt her paw.

5 The ____ bleated as the dog rounded them up.

6 The boys were up before the ____ started crowing.

7 Robert's brown ____ clucked after laying an egg.

8 The ____ grunted as he ate his food.

Verbs

I **like** apples.

Sally **likes** apples.

We both **like** apples.

I, you, we, they	**he, she, it**
do	does
go	goes
put	puts
run	runs
pull	pulls
play	plays
say	says
try	tries
carry	carries
hurry	hurries

A Copy and fill in the missing verb.

1 they ____ **go** **goes**

2 I ____ **try** **tries**

3 he ____ **pull** **pulls**

4 you ____ **say** **says**

5 we ____ **do** **does**

6 she ____ **put** **puts**

7 you ____ **hurry** **hurries**

8 it ____ **run** **runs**

9 I ____ **carry** **carries**

10 they ____ **play** **plays**

B Write the verb from the list on the left which will fill each space correctly.

1 The children ____ football every day.

2 Mr. Gold ____ his umbrella on his arm.

3 Judith ____ her knitting by the fire.

4 We ____ to school five days a week.

5 Peter ____ his prayers every night.

6 I will catch the bus if I ____ .

7 Our cat always ____ after a mouse.

8 Sheila ____ hard to write a good letter.

C Write sentences of your own showing how each of these words can be used.

1 make makes

2 eat eats

3 read reads

4 think thinks

5 walk walks

6 learn learns

Writing letters

A Read the letter which Tom Weller wrote to his friend Brian Baxter inviting him to his birthday party. Tom's mother showed him how to arrange the letter and how to address the envelope.
Notice the postcode HD24 3PX. Always show the postcode in the last line of your address.

Pretend you are Brian Baxter and that you have just had this letter from Tom Weller.

Write a letter to him thanking him for his kind invitation and telling him that you will be delighted to come.

Draw an envelope and address it to Tom. You will find his address at the top of his letter.

B Pretend that you have been to Tom's party. Write a letter to another friend who was not there telling him how much you enjoyed yourself. Say what you had to eat, what games you played and what fireworks you saw.

Draw an envelope and address it to your friend.

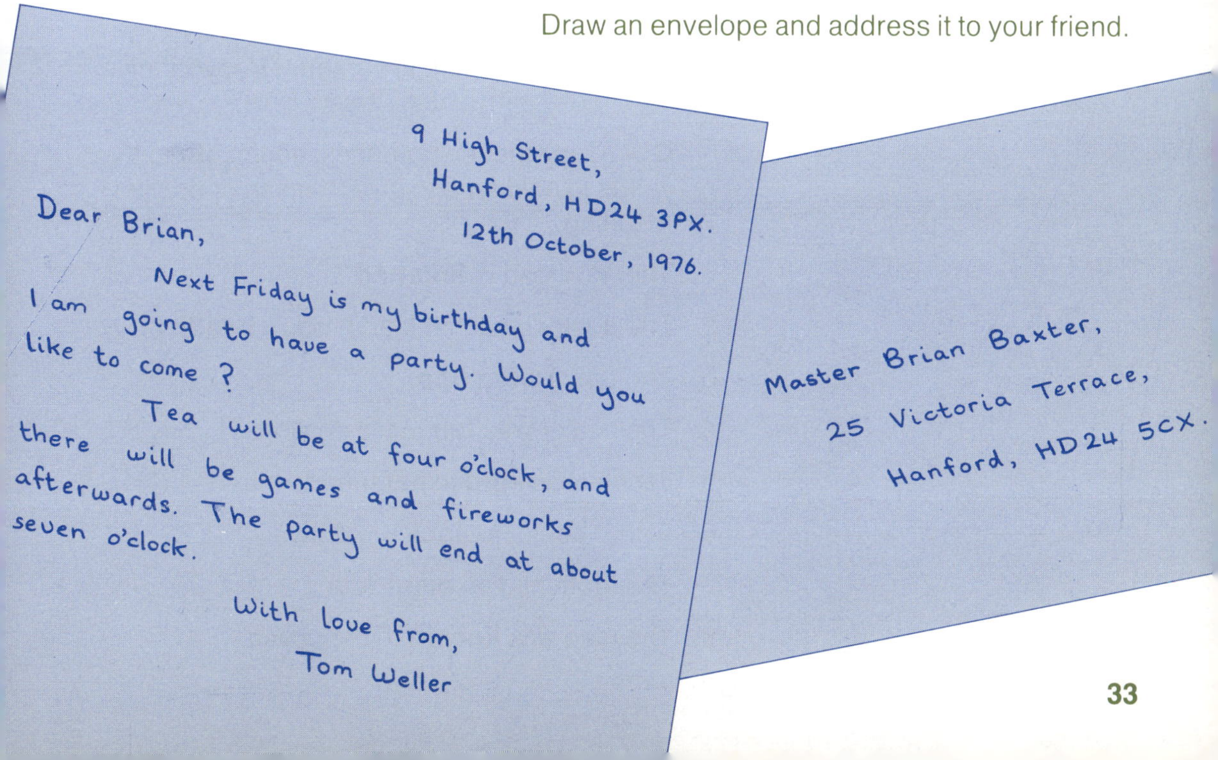

9 High Street,
Hanford, HD24 3PX.
12th October, 1976.

Dear Brian,

Next Friday is my birthday and I am going to have a party. Would you like to come?

Tea will be at four o'clock, and there will be games and fireworks afterwards. The party will end at about seven o'clock.

With love from,
Tom Weller

Master Brian Baxter,
25 Victoria Terrace,
Hanford, HD24 5CX.

Opposites using un

safe **unsafe**

Some words are given an opposite meaning by writing **un** before them.

Look at the words above the pictures.

A Form the opposites of these words by using **un**.

1	happy	5	do	9	roll
2	willing	6	screw	10	real
3	paid	7	tie	11	safe
4	seen	8	wise	12	steady

B Choose any six of the words you have made and use them in sentences of your own.

C Copy these sentences, adding **un** to the words in bold type to give them an opposite meaning.

1 The new road is **finished**.

2 The doctor said that Martin was a **healthy** boy.

3 The pears were **ripe**.

4 The dealer was **fair** in his dealings.

5 Jennie was **kind** to her friends.

6 Father could not **lock** the drawer.

7 The room had an **even** floor.

8 The man was **known** to the police.

Collections

A number of **sheep** together is called a **flock**.

A number of **tools** together is called a **set**.

a bunch of grapes
a chest of drawers
a crowd of people
a flight of steps
a flock of birds
a herd of cattle
a pack of wolves
a pair of shoes
a suit of clothes
a shoal of fish

A Write the missing words. You will find them in the list on the left.

1	a ____ of people	6	a flight of ____
2	a ____ of wolves	7	a chest of ____
3	a ____ of grapes	8	a shoal of ____
4	a ____ of shoes	9	a herd of ____
5	a ____ of clothes	10	a flock of ____

B Write the word which will fill each gap.

1 A ____ of steps led to the cabin.

2 A large ____ of starlings flew over the town.

3 Our milk comes from a ____ of Jersey cows.

4 A pack of ____ went hunting in the forest.

5 A ____ of fish swam past our boat.

6 A ____ of people gathered to welcome the Prince.

7 The clothes were kept in an old ____ of drawers.

8 She bought a new ____ of shoes for the wedding.

9 Father gave his old ____ of clothes to a jumble sale.

10 When my aunt was in hospital my uncle took her a lovely ____ of black grapes.

Tom Thumb

The woodman took his family into a very thick wood where they could not see one another ten paces off. The woodman began to cut some wood, and the children to gather up the sticks and to make them into bundles. Their father and mother, seeing them all so busy, crept away from them bit by bit, and then all at once ran away through the bushes.

When the children saw that they had been left alone they started to cry loudly. Tom Thumb let them cry, for he had taken care to drop all along the road the little white stones he had in his pockets.

Then he said to them, "Do not be afraid, brothers. Father and Mother have left us here, but I will take you home again; only follow me."

They followed him, and he brought them home through the wood by the same road as they had come.

Tales from Perrault

1. Where did the woodman take his family?
2. What did he do when they got there?
3. How did the children help their father?
4. What did the father and mother do when the children were busy?
5. Why did the children start to cry?
6. Why did Tom let them cry?
7. What had Tom done on the way to the wood?
8. How was Tom able to take his brothers home again?

Group names

The **robin** is a **bird**. So is the **sparrow** and so is the **thrush**.

They all belong to the same **group**. They are all **birds**.

animals
flowers
dogs
fruits
colours
insects
days
tools
fish
trees

A Use a group name from the list on the left to finish each sentence.

1 Oak, ash, birch and elm are all ____ .

2 Terrier, corgi, spaniel and collie are all ____ .

3 Hammer, saw, pincers and chisel are all ____ .

4 Monday, Thursday, Friday and Tuesday are all ____ .

5 Herring, cod, hake and haddock are all ____ .

6 Fly, wasp, bee and gnat are all ____ .

7 Lion, tiger, bear and wolf are all ____ .

8 Red, blue, yellow and green are all ____ .

9 Rose, lily, tulip and crocus are all ____ .

10 Pear, apple, plum and banana are all ____ .

B In each column below there is one word which does not belong to the same group as the others.
Write the odd word.

1 willow, oak, birch, daffodil, beech

2 blue, bright, black, yellow, green

3 apple, orange, turnip, lemon, pear

4 cow, goat, sheep, moth, horse

5 Christmas, Friday, Wednesday, Monday, Thursday

6 violet, dandelion, bluebell, mushroom, snowdrop

People who work

A Use the words in the list on the left to name each person. Number your words 1 to 8 as in the pictures.

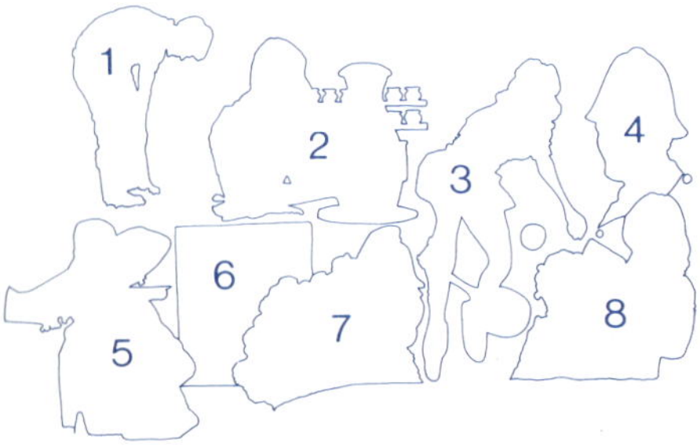

stewardess	fishmonger
fireman	hairdresser
farmer	potter
teacher	policeman
porter	window cleaner
guard	tennis player
sailor	gardener
soldier	

B Write the missing words. The list on the left will help you.

1 I asked the ____ when the plane was going to land.

2 The ____ had some fine fillets of hake.

3 The ____ is giving an arithmetic lesson.

4 The ____ wheeled Martin's trunk to the luggage van.

5 Jane has gone to the ____ to have her hair cut.

6 The ____ blew his whistle and the train moved off.

7 The ____ went aboard the battleship.

8 We watched the ____ cutting the hay.

9 The ____ on sentry duty carried a rifle.

10 A big crowd saw the ____ rescue the boy from the burning house.

The doers of actions

The person who **teaches** you is your **teacher**.
Teach is the action.
Teacher is the **doer** of the action.

A Add **-er** to each of these verbs to make the name of the doer.

1	help	4	bowl	7	clean
2	jump	5	read	8	dream
3	lead	6	sleep		

B Before adding **-er** to these words, double the last letter.

1	run	4	win	7	trap
2	rob	5	drum	8	travel
3	shop	6	swim		

C Drop the **e** when you add **-er** to these words.

1	ride	3	drive	5	strike
2	dance	4	lodge	6	write

D Change **y** to **i** before adding **-er**.

1	cry	3	dry	5	carry
2	fly	4	copy	6	supply

E Write the words which fill the spaces.

1 Andrew was a strong ____. **swim**

2 The ____ could not keep in step with his partner. **dance**

3 Louise is a very quick ____. **read**

4 The ____ was given a gold medal. **win**

5 He has been a ____ at that house for ten years. **lodge**

6 The ____ sent two parcels to the school. **supply**

7 Our ____ keeps the school very tidy. **clean**

8 A policeman stopped the ____ of the sports car. **drive**

Male and female

A **boy** is a **he**, or a **male**.
A **man** is a **he**, or a **male**.

A **girl** is a **she**, or a **female**.
A **woman** is a **she**, or a **female**.

Male	**Female**
actor	actress
cockerel	hen
dog	bitch
gander	goose
grandfather	grandmother
master	mistress
prince	princess
son	daughter
tiger	tigress
waiter	waitress

A Copy this column, then write the missing words.

	Male	**Female**
1	____	princess
2	grandfather	____
3	____	daughter
4	waiter	____
5	gander	____
6	____	bitch
7	____	tigress
8	____	actress
9	cockerel	____
10	____	mistress

B Change **male** nouns to **female**, and **female** to **male**.

1 The waitress took our order and left.

2 The actor tripped over the scenery and fell on his face.

3 The goose hissed at the children.

4 The master of the house was out.

5 The teacher's son was very ill.

6 The hunter shot the huge tiger.

7 The old hen scratched in the earth for worms.

8 In the evening the prince walked in the garden.

Animals

A Write the names of these animals.

bear
fox
lion
camel
donkey
giraffe
hedgehog
elephant
kangaroo
squirrel

B Write the name of the animal which will complete each sentence. You will find them in the list on the left.

1 The _____ is covered with sharp spines and can roll itself into a ball when attacked.

2 The _____ has a long trunk and strong tusks.

3 The _____ has a hump on its back and can carry people and goods across the desert.

4 The _____ has a spotted skin and a very long neck.

5 The _____ has a bushy tail which curls over its back.

6 The _____ is a cunning animal which steals chickens.

7 The _____ is called the King of Beasts. Its loud roar frightens many animals.

8 The _____ is a stubborn animal with very long ears. It is sometimes called an ass.

9 The _____ has strong hind legs which enable it to move forward in great leaps.

10 A _____ has a shaggy coat and strong claws. It can hug a person to death.

The fox and the goat

While reaching down to drink the water in a well one day, a fox fell in. Try as he would, he could not get out again because the walls of the well were too high.

Not long after, a goat came along. Seeing the fox down there, he asked him the reason why.

"I am enjoying the cool, pure water," replied the fox. "Wouldn't you like to jump down and taste it?"

Without stopping to think, the foolish old goat jumped down. No sooner had he reached the bottom than the cunning old fox leaped on to his back and scrambled to the top.

Looking down at the unhappy goat the fox laughed and said, "Next time, friend goat, be sure to look before you leap."

Aesop's Fables

1 What did the fox have to do before he could drink the water in the well?
2 What happened to him while he was doing this?
3 Why could he not get out of the well?
4 What did the goat ask the fox?
5 What was the answer given by the fox?
6 What did the goat do when the fox asked him to try the water?
7 How did the fox get to the top again?
8 What did he tell the goat to do the next time?

Adverbs

Andrew tiptoed **quietly** from the room.

The word **quietly** tells how he left the room.

This word is formed by adding **-ly** to quiet.

A Add **-ly** to each of these words.

quick	safe	kind
calm	neat	fond
sad	quiet	proud

B When **-ly** is added to words ending with **y**, this letter is first changed to **i**.

Examples

clumsy	clumsily
hasty	hastily

Add **-ly** to these words.

easy	lucky	greedy
busy	heavy	hungry
sleepy	angry	
noisy	steady	

C The word which fills each space below is formed by adding **-ly** to the word in bold type. Write the nine words.

1 The flames spread so ____ that the house was soon burnt to the ground. **quick**

2 All the boys were working ____. **busy**

3 The ship arrived ____ after a stormy voyage. **safe**

4 The snail crept ____ along the garden path. **slow**

5 The old man nodded his head ____. **sleepy**

6 It is raining too ____ for you to go out. **heavy**

7 The young mother looked ____ at her baby. **proud**

8 Sandra wrote the letter very ____. **neat**

9 Philip jumped over the wall quite ____. **easy**

Opposites change of word

Look at this list of opposites, then answer the questions.

back	front
buy	sell
glad	sorry
bitter	sweet
dark	light
long	short
poor	rich
break	mend
fast	slow
noisy	quiet

A Use the opposite of the word in bold type to fill each space.

Example a fast train **slow**

1 to ____ a rabbit **buy**

2 a ____ room **dark**

3 a ____ seat **back**

4 a ____ story **long**

5 a ____ orange **sweet**

6 a ____ street **quiet**

7 a ____ man **poor**

8 to ____ a toy **break**

9 to be ____ **glad**

B Fill each gap with the opposite of the word in bold type.

1 If you ____ your arm it will take about six weeks to **mend**.

2 We are going to paint the **front** and the ____ of our house.

3 He was ____ when his cousin came but **sorry** when he left.

4 Uncle will **sell** his old car and ____ a new one.

5 He tied the ____ length of cord to the **long** one.

6 The children were **quiet** in school but very ____ outside.

7 Ten years ago he was ____. Now he is very **rich**.

8 He wore a **dark** grey suit and a ____ grey hat.

9 The clock was five minutes **fast** yesterday but it is ____ today.

Group names

An apple is
a **fruit**.

A cabbage is
a **vegetable**.

A rose is
a **flower**.

A teddy bear is
a **toy**.

bird
fish
toy
tree
tool
fruit
flower
insect
animal
vegetable

A Write the group name for each of these objects.

1 A doll is a ____ .

2 A peach is a ____ .

3 A herring is a ____ .

4 An oak is a ____ .

5 A tiger is an ____ .

6 A wasp is an ____ .

7 A turnip is a ____ .

8 A crocus is a ____ .

9 A sparrow is a ____ .

10 A hammer is a ____ .

B Draw four columns in your book, like these. Then put the words below in their correct columns.

Fruits	**Fishes**	**Vegetables**	**Tools**

parsnip	cabbage	trowel	plum
rake	lemon	mackerel	salmon
orange	plaice	beetroot	onion
carrot	spade	banana	hatchet
herring	apricot	spanner	hake

Food and drink

Copy these sentences. Use the words in the list below to fill the spaces.

bacon	margarine
beef	marmalade
breakfast	milk
butter	mutton
cereals	pork
cream	pudding
eggs	sugar
flour	wheat

A

1 Bread, buns and cakes are made from ____ .

2 Flour is a fine meal or powder made from ____ .

3 Many children have cornflakes, puffed wheat and similar foods for ____ .

4 Such foods are known as ____ .

5 The ____ we eat are laid by hens.

6 Butter, eggs and sugar are used with rice to make a rice ____ .

7 Fruit is boiled with ____ to make jam.

8 Jam made with oranges is called ____ .

B

1 The ____ which we drink comes from the cow.

2 If milk is allowed to stand the ____ rises to the top.

3 The ____ which we spread on our bread is made from milk.

4 Many people eat ____ instead of butter.

5 The meat we get from the cow is called ____ .

6 The meat from a pig is known as ____ .

7 ____ is the meat we get from the sheep.

8 ____ is the flesh of a pig salted and sometimes smoked.

Alphabetical order

All these words begin with a different letter.

fruit
year
march
board
shade

To put them in **a-b-c** or alphabetical order we look at the first letter only.

board
fruit
march
shade
year

All these words begin with the same letter.

bead
black
brick
book
bath

To put them in alphabetical order we must look at the **second** letter in each.

e l r o a

Now it is easy to put them in their right order.

b**a**th
b**e**ad
b**l**ack
b**o**ok
b**r**ick

A Write the words in each column in alphabetical order.

1	2	3
bank	crop	loaf
bend	club	lick
boat	case	lump
bite	chop	lamb
burn	cost	leaf

4	5	6
peck	slot	much
part	scar	milk
port	ship	meat
pure	stop	mask
pine	safe	more

B Can you spot the word which is **out of order** in each of these columns?

1	2	3
nail	gate	feel
near	glad	fine
nice	give	from
nurse	gone	flat
noon	grow	fuss

4	5
echo	pill
east	plan
edge	pray
else	post
even	punt

The lion and the mouse

A lion was asleep in his den one day when a playful little mouse ran up his outstretched paw and across his nose awakening him from his nap. As quick as lightning the lion clapped his mighty paw upon the frightened little mouse and roared angrily.

"Please don't kill me," squealed the mouse. "Forgive me this time and I will never forget it. One day I may be able to do you a good turn to repay your kindness."

The lion smiled at the mouse, amused by the thought that such a tiny creature could ever be able to help him. So he lifted his paw and let the mouse go.

Later, while the lion was out hunting, he became caught in a net which some men had set to catch him. At once he let out a roar that echoed through the forest. The little mouse heard it, and recognising the voice of the lion who had spared his life, ran to where the king of beasts lay tangled in the net of ropes.

"Well, your majesty," said the mouse, "I know you did not believe me when I said that a day may come when I may repay your kindness, but here is my chance."

At once the little mouse started to nibble through the ropes that bound the lion with his sharp little teeth. Soon the lion was free and able to crawl out of the hunters' snare.

This fable teaches us that no act of kindness, however small, is ever wasted.

1. What was the lion doing in his den?
2. What did the playful little mouse do to the lion?
3. What did the lion do to the mouse?
4. Why was the mouse so frightened?
5. What did the mouse ask the lion to do?
6. Why was the lion so amused at what the mouse said?
7. What happened when the lion was out hunting?
8. How did the mouse set the lion free?
9. What does this fable teach us?
10. What is the lion sometimes called?

Verbs past time

Present time
We **begin** our holidays today.

Past time
They **began** their holidays yesterday.

Learn the verbs in this list, then answer the questions.

Present	**Past**
blow	blew
break	broke
do	did
drive	drove
eat	ate
feel	felt
fly	flew
hide	hid
know	knew
sleep	slept
take	took
tear	tore

A Copy this column. Fill the blanks.

	Present	**Past**
1	tear	____
2	break	____
3	sleep	____
4	know	____
5	____	took
6	____	hid
7	____	drove
8	____	ate
9	fly	____
10	____	blew
11	do	____
12	____	felt

B Write the words which must be used to fill the gaps.

1 Peter ____ a long time to do his sums.

2 Mr. Bond ____ the car into the garage.

3 I went to bed early and ____ all night.

4 The high wind ____ the leaves off the trees.

5 Barbara ____ a plate when she washed the dishes.

6 The dog ____ all his food and begged for more.

7 The lark ____ up into the sky.

8 James ____ a pain in his side.

9 Martin ____ the answer to every question.

10 Anne ____ her skirt on a rusty nail.

Birthdays

A Read this poem, then answer the questions.

Monday's child is fair of face,
Tuesday's child is full of grace,
Wednesday's child is full of woe,
Thursday's child has far to go,
Friday's child is loving and giving,
Saturday's child works hard for its living,
But the child that is born on a Sunday
Is fair and wise and good and gay.

1 Which child has to work hard for a living?
2 The child born on a Tuesday is full of ____.
3 Which child will be a sad child?
4 Which child will be a pretty child?
5 Which child is loving and giving?
6 Which child will travel a lot?
7 What is the child born on a Sunday like?

B Write the names of the days of the week in order.

Opposite each day write a sentence about something you do on that day.

Examples

Monday	I take money to school to pay for my dinners for the week.
Tuesday	I borrow a book from the class library.
Saturday	I go shopping with Mother.

Same sound — different meaning

Some words have the same sound as other words, but they differ in spelling and meaning.

Look at these four pairs of words.
Learn to spell each word.
Learn the meaning of each.

hear	You **hear** with your ears.
here	I will wait **here** for you. (*in this place*)
main	The **main** road is the most important one.
mane	The long hair on the neck of a horse or a lion is called a **mane**.
meat	The flesh of an animal used for food is called **meat**.
meet	When people **meet** they get together.
pail	A **pail** is a kind of bucket.
pale	A **pale** person has little colour.

Choose the correct word from the pair above to complete each sentence.

1 **pail** **pale**
She looked very _____ after her illness.

2 **meat** **meet**
The _____ was too tough to eat.

3 **here** **hear**
We did not _____ the postman knocking.

4 **main** **mane**
The school is on the _____ road.

5 **pail** **pale**
The _____ was half full of water.

6 **main** **mane**
The horse had a very long _____ .

7 **meat** **meet**
We will _____ you outside the cinema.

The months of the year

January

S		6	13	20	27
M		7	14	21	28
T	1	8	15	22	29
W	2	9	16	23	30
Th	3	10	17	24	31
F	4	11	18	25	
S	5	12	19	26	

February

S		3	10	17	24
M		4	11	18	25
T		5	12	19	26
W		6	13	20	27
Th		7	14	21	28
F	1	8	15	22	29
S	2	9	16	23	

March

S		2	9	16	23	30
M		3	10	17	24	31
T		4	11	18	25	
W		5	12	19	26	
Th		6	13	20	27	
F		7	14	21	28	
S	1	8	15	22	29	

April

S		6	13	20	27
M		7	14	21	28
T	1	8	15	22	29
W	2	9	16	23	30
Th	3	10	17	24	
F	4	11	18	25	
S	5	12	19	26	

May

S		4	11	18	25
M		5	12	19	26
T		6	13	20	27
W		7	14	21	28
Th	1	8	15	22	29
F	2	9	16	23	30
S	3	10	17	24	31

June

S	1	8	15	22	29
M	2	9	16	23	30
T	3	10	17	24	
W	4	11	18	25	
Th	5	12	19	26	
F	6	13	20	27	
S	7	14	21	28	

July

S		6	13	20	27
M		7	14	21	28
T	1	8	15	22	29
W	2	9	16	23	30
Th	3	10	17	24	31
F	4	11	18	25	
S	5	12	19	26	

August

S		3	10	17	24	31
M		4	11	18	25	
T		5	12	19	26	
W		6	13	20	27	
Th		7	14	21	28	
F	1	8	15	22	29	
S	2	9	16	23	30	

September

S		7	14	21	28
M	1	8	15	22	29
T	2	9	16	23	30
W	3	10	17	24	
Th	4	11	18	25	
F	5	12	19	26	
S	6	13	20	27	

October

S		5	12	19	26
M		6	13	20	27
T		7	14	21	28
W	1	8	15	22	29
Th	2	9	16	23	30
F	3	10	17	24	31
S	4	11	18	25	

November

S		2	9	16	23	30
M		3	10	17	24	
T		4	11	18	25	
W		5	12	19	26	
Th		6	13	20	27	
F		7	14	21	28	
S	1	8	15	22	29	

December

S		7	14	21	28
M	1	8	15	22	29
T	2	9	16	23	30
W	3	10	17	24	31
Th	4	11	18	25	
F	5	12	19	26	
S	6	13	20	27	

A Look at the calendar. Answer the questions. A year in which February has 29 days is known as a Leap Year.

1. How many months are there in the year?
2. Which month has the shortest name?
3. Write the names of the three months ending with **-ember**.
4. Which month has the longest name?
5. Which month has fewest days?
6. In which month does your birthday come?
7. Name the month in which Christmas comes.
8. Write the names of the four months which have no letter **r** in them.

B We can write the names of most of the months in a short way.

Copy these short forms and learn them.

1	January	Jan.
2	February	Feb.
3	March	Mar.
4	April	April
5	May	May
6	June	June
7	July	July
8	August	Aug.
9	September	Sept.
10	October	Oct.
11	November	Nov.
12	December	Dec.

Writing dates

Write **st** after the number.

1st first

21st twenty-first

31st thirty-first

Write **nd** after the number.

2nd second

22nd twenty-second

Write **rd** after the number.

3rd third

23rd twenty-third

For all other numbers in the calender add **th**.

4th fourth

11th eleventh

17th seventeenth

25th twenty-fifth

A Use numbers to write these.

1	fifth	6	third	11	thirty-first
2	tenth	7	ninth	12	seventh
3	second	8	twenty-first	13	twenty-third
4	first	9	sixteenth	14	twelfth
5	sixth	10	fourth	15	twenty-second

B **Writing dates**: 14th May or May 14th

1. Write the date for the twenty-fourth of September.
2. On which date does New Year's Day come?
3. What is the date today?
4. Write the date of your birthday.
5. Write the date for August the twenty-first.
6. On which date does Christmas Day come?

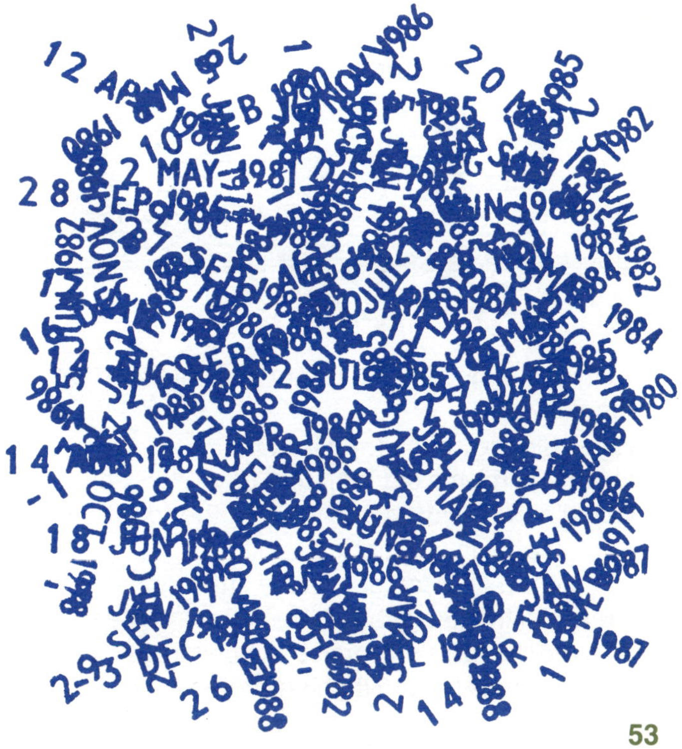

A camping holiday

Last summer Roger and his sister Jill went on a camping holiday in Wales with their parents for the first time. Their new blue tent, which had two bedrooms and a living-room, was pitched in a large field near a sandy bay. There were no other tents in the field and Roger pretended that they were explorers.

Early every morning the two children and their mother went swimming while their father made the breakfast. When they came back, hungry from their exercise, they found him frying bacon and eggs on a portable gas stove. After breakfast they all went down to the beach and played cricket and enjoyed the sunshine.

In the afternoons the children went fishing with their nets in the clear pools, while their parents sat on the sand reading. In the evening they walked to the farmhouse at the foot of the hill. They watched the cows being milked and then had supper with the farmer and his wife. The farmer told the children all about his animals and his crops and promised to let them help with the harvest if they came back in the autumn. At sunset they strolled back along the deserted road to their tent, climbed into their sleeping bags and fell fast asleep. Nothing disturbed them until the singing of the birds woke them next morning.

1 What kind of holiday did Roger and Jill have last summer?
2 Where did they pitch their tent?
3 How many rooms did their tent have?
4 What did the children and their mother do while their father was preparing breakfast?
5 How did the children spend the afternoons?
6 Where did the family have their evening meal?
7 What did the farmer promise the children?
8 What awakened them in the morning?

Rhymes

A Read this poem carefully. Then copy it, putting in the words which you think will end each line.

car star bar tar
far jar are war
lie nigh shy high
sly pie sky sty

let set bet net
pet met wet yet
tight fight sight light
right night might white

Twinkle, twinkle, little ____,
How I wonder what you ____!
Up above the world so ____
Like a diamond in the ____.

When the blazing sun is ____,
And the grass with dew is ____,
Then you show your little ____,
Twinkle, twinkle, all the ____.

B Write the list of words in capital letters. After each word write the three words in small letters which will rhyme with it.

Example 1 LATE gate, weight, wait

1	LATE	mend	park	stout
2	BARK	gate	pout	sing
3	OUT	cling	weight	lend
4	BEND	mark	about	bring
5	RING	wait	lark	send

C The missing word in each line below rhymes with the word in bold type.

1 Two pence is a ____ sum of money. **crawl**

2 I will ____ you at the corner of the street. **heat**

3 The bread was too ____ to eat. **nail**

4 If you ____ a dog he may bite you. **these**

5 Mother asked Sally to ____ the tea. **snore**

Compound words

A **compound** word is formed by joining together two or more words

Example
tea+pot=teapot

A Write the name of each object. Show the two words which make up each compound word.

Example
1 **rail+way=railway**

armchair
wheelbarrow
birdcage
matchbox
butterfly
silkworm
cowboy
bulldog
hedgehog
snowdrop
dustbin
greenhouse
broomstick

B In each line below, join together the two words in bold type to form a compound word. Start with the second word.

1 a **fish** which is **gold** in colour
2 a **boat** which is driven by a **motor**
3 a **stand** on which a **band** plays
4 a **cloth** which covers a **table**
5 a **ball** made of **snow**
6 a **room** for a **bed**
7 **weed** which grows in the **sea**
8 a **tray** to hold cigarette **ash**
9 a **box** for keeping **cash**
10 a **coat** which is worn **over** all other clothes

The long and the short

There is a short way of writing some words.

Avenue	Ave.
Doctor	Dr.
Mistress	Mrs.
Mister	Mr.
Road	Rd.
Square	Sq.
Street	St.
Terrace	Terr.

A Write each of these the short way:

1 Doctor Smith
2 High Street
3 Mister Lee
4 Station Terrace
5 Mistress Bond
6 Bush Avenue
7 Victoria Square
8 Redlands Road

Initials

Instead of writing a person's first or Christian name or names in full we write only the **first letter**, as a **capital**, followed by a full stop.

Examples

Edward Marsh
E. Marsh

Arthur John Bond
A. J. Bond

B Draw envelopes in your exercise book and write these names and addresses, using initials and the short forms you have learnt.

1 Mister Ronald Green, of 12 Church Street, Camford, CP20 3NF.

2 Mistress Jane Everson, of 9 Norton Road, Benham, BP13 4QT.

3 Miss Eva May Brent, of 16 Park Terrace, Broxley, BI58 2RV.

4 Doctor David Alan Johnson, of 23 Poplar Avenue, Reddington, RN41 9GH.

5 Mister William Frederick Dixon, of 31 Chester Square, Podworth, PE57 9AL.

Short forms

The short way of writing **has not** is **hasn't**.
We can also write **that is** a short way – **that's**.

In a similar way the word **will** can be added to words and written in a short way.

I will	I'll
you will	you'll
he will	he'll
she will	she'll
we will	we'll
they will	they'll

Remember that the **'** shows that the letters **wi** have been left out.

A Write the short form for:

1	is not	6	do not	11	I will
2	we will	7	where is	12	does not
3	here is	8	you will	13	it is
4	he will	9	did not	14	she will
5	are not	10	they will	15	what is

B Write the short form of the two words in bold type in these sentences.

1 I know **you will** be pleased with your present.

2 Peter says **there is** plenty of time.

3 Next time **we will** go by train.

4 We must find out **who is** going to the party.

5 I promise you **I will** do my best.

6 If Barbara is late **she will** be scolded.

7 The boys say **they will** call on their way home.

8 Alan **would not** get up when called.

9 Very likely **he will** be late for school.

10 Everybody says **it is** a fine drawing.

Similars

A **plucky** sailor

A **brave** sailor

The words **plucky** and **brave** are similar in meaning.

Learn the list of similars, then answer the questions.

aged	old
connect	join
glance	look
loiter	linger
slender	slim
cash	money
garments	clothes
handsome	beautiful
plump	fat
tremble	shake

A For each word in bold type give a word which has a similar meaning.

1 The **cash** was taken to the bank.

2 The plumber came to **connect** the pipes.

3 He is a very **handsome** child.

4 The Browns had a **plump** goose for Christmas.

5 You should not **loiter** on the way home.

6 He did not even **glance** at the book.

7 The dancer had a **slender** figure.

8 The door was opened by an **aged** servant.

9 The trains made the old bridge **tremble**.

10 All **garments** sold in this shop are tailor made.

B Write simpler words which are similar in meaning to these. Some you learnt in Book 1.

1	broad	9	commence
2	plucky	10	reply
3	finish	11	wealthy
4	large	12	weeping
5	repair	13	correct
6	collect	14	peril
7	difficult	15	assist
8	stout	16	farewell

Androcles and the lion

Once, long ago, a shepherd was roaming the hot, desert land of Africa when he met a lion. He was very frightened, but when he saw that the lion had a thorn in its paw and was in terrible pain he walked towards it, spoke to it gently and pulled out the thorn. From that time on, Androcles and the lion were great friends.

Some time later some soldiers came and arrested Androcles. They took him far across the sea to the great city of Rome. The Emperor of Rome tried to make Androcles give up his Christian faith, and when he refused had him thrown into a huge arena to be torn apart and eaten by a fierce lion.

Androcles saw the lion spring towards him. Then, suddenly, the lion stopped, bowed its head and held out its paw. Androcles knew then that this lion was his friend from the desert of Africa who had been captured by hunters and brought to Rome.

The Emperor was amazed. "You and your lion have been loyal and brave, Androcles," he said. "You shall both be released at once."

So Androcles and the lion returned across the sea to their home in the desert land of Africa.

1 In which country did Androcles meet the lion?
2 What work did Androcles do for his living?
3 How did Androcles feel when he first saw the lion?
4 What did the Roman Emperor want Androcles to do?
5 How did the Romans punish Christians who would not give up their faith?
6 Why did the Emperor release Androcles and the lion?
7 Where did they go when they were released?
8 Androcles was loyal and brave. Write a sentence to say what else you think he was.

Fun with words

In each group of words on the right are two pairs of words and one odd word.

You have to find the word which will make up the third pair.

Look at the first pair of words in **A**: **ten** **tent**.

The second word is made by writing the letter **t** after the first word.

Look at the second pair. The second word is again formed by writing **t** after the first word: **sea** **seat**.

To find the missing word write **t** after the odd word.

Example **star** **start**

A Now find the other missing words. In each group a different letter must be added.

1 ten tent
sea seat
star

2 pan pane
hop hope
hid

3 bun bung
ran rang
thin

4 ten tend
ban band
win

5 tea team
for form
war

B From the letters in the word **tens** we can make the word **nest**.

From the letters in the words in bold type make words which will fit into the spaces below.

1 There were five eggs in the _____ . **tens**

2 The performing bear was quite _____ . **meat**

3 The journey was a very _____ one. **owls**

4 Every child should learn to _____ well. **dare**

5 We should take great _____ with our spelling. **race**

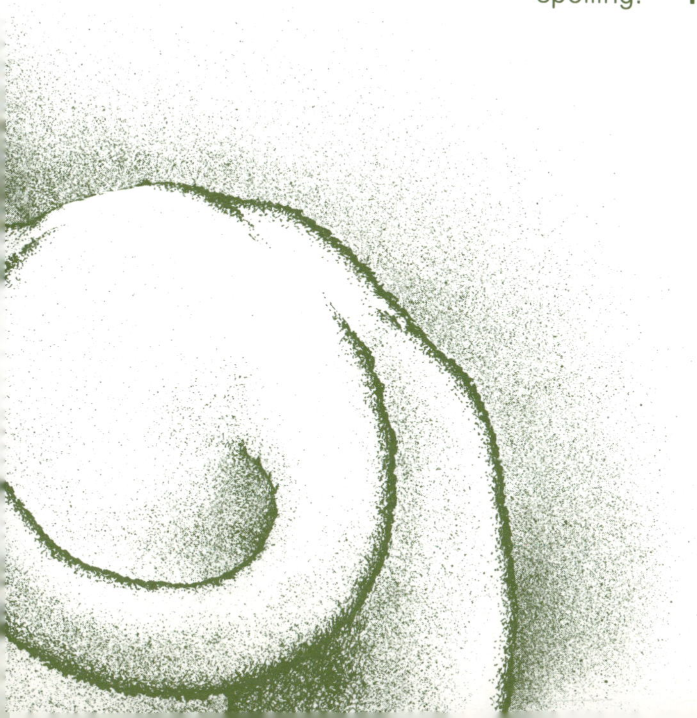

More fun with words

A Each dash in these sentences stands for a letter.
Each group of letters spells a word.

Example
Mary has long g_ _ _en hair.
The missing letters are **old**.

Each missing word has **three** letters. Write the missing words only.

1 The plants were bl_ _ _ down by the strong wind.

2 Pigs g_ _ _t when they eat their food.

3 The little boy sat down on the three-legged s_ _ _l.

4 We sometimes have snow in the _ _ _ter.

5 Wolves were h_ _ _ing in the forest.

6 The _ _ _tain of the ship was a Dane.

7 The mon_ _ _ hung from the tree by his long tail.

B Each missing word has **four** letters. Write the missing words only.

1 Wendy's class will have a new t_ _ _ _er next term.

2 Bees had s_ _ _ _ed on an apple tree in the garden.

3 The tired horse was taken to the st_ _ _ _.

4 Mother lit the fire because the room was c_ _ _ _y.

5 The engine was letting off s_ _ _ _.

6 We saw the p_ _ _ _ landing on the runway.

7 The express t_ _ _ _ ran off the rails.

Verbs past time

Present time:
I **feel** a pain in my side today.

Past time:
I **felt** a pain in my side yesterday.

Learn the words in this list, then answer the questions.

Present	Past
build	built
creep	crept
grow	grew
ride	rode
ring	rang
rise	rose
see	saw
sink	sank
speak	spoke
steal	stole

A Copy this column. Fill the blanks.

	Present	Past
1	____	saw
2	____	rang
3	____	rose
4	____	grew
5	____	sank
6	speak	____
7	steal	____
8	ride	____
9	build	____
10	creep	____

B Write the words which will fill the gaps.

1 He ____ to the seaside on his new bicycle.
2 The boat filled with water and ____ .
3 The boy ____ the school bell.
4 The gardener ____ some beautiful roses.
5 I ____ to him on the telephone.
6 The boys ____ a sandcastle on the beach.
7 We ____ two bear cubs in the zoo.
8 The thief ____ the money from the till.
9 The sun ____ at six o'clock yesterday morning.
10 The burglar ____ quietly into the house.

Using took and taken

I **took** a book home.

I **have taken** a book home.

(**have** helps the word **taken**)

The book **was taken** home

(**was** helps the word **taken**)

The word **took** needs no helping word.

The word **taken** always has a helping word:

is taken
was taken
are taken
were taken
has taken
have taken
had taken
will be taken

A Use **took** or **taken** to fill each space.

1 It was ____
2 You ____
3 He has ____
4 I ____
5 They are ____
6 You have ____
7 He ____
8 We were ____
9 It will be ____
10 She ____

B Fill each space with **took** or **taken**.

1 The man was ____ ill at the football match.
2 They ____ the man to the hospital.
3 Susan ____ her cocoa to bed with her.
4 She ____ two pills after dinner.
5 The thief ____ all the money in the house.
6 Jean has ____ great care with her work.
7 The two men were ____ to prison.
8 After Alan had ____ his shoes to the shoe repairer he went fishing.
9 As it was raining father ____ his umbrella.
10 The dustmen have ____ the rubbish away.

When people speak

Look at this sentence:

"This orange is sour," said Robert.

The words spoken by Robert were
This orange is sour.

Notice the speech marks come before the first word spoken **"This** . . . and after the last word spoken . . . **sour,"**

Notice that the speech marks come after the comma:
. . . **sour,"**

The speech marks would also come after a question mark:

"Is the orange sour?" asked Robert.

A Copy these sentences. Put in the speech marks.

1 Pass me the sugar, please, said Mrs. Norland.

2 Are you tired? asked the teacher.

3 I can see you, shouted Brian.

4 Please, Mummy, may I have an apple? begged Simon.

5 Come here, Spot, said the little boy to his dog.

6 I don't want to go to bed yet, said Sandra with a pout.

7 Hurry up, Linda, or you'll be late, said her mother.

8 Spare a penny for the guy, please? asked the two boys.

9 Here is fifty pence for you, replied the gentleman.

10 Be quiet, baby's sleeping, whispered Jennifer's mother.

B Write three sentences of your own in which there are words spoken by people.

John and the cherries

One day John went shopping with his mother. Their first call was at the greengrocer's, and while his mother was buying some fruit John looked longingly at a box containing lovely red cherries.

"Help yourself to a handful, John," said the greengrocer, but John did not move.

"I'm sure you like cherries, don't you?" asked the puzzled shopkeeper, and John nodded his head quickly. Thinking that the boy was too shy to help himself the greengrocer went to the box and gave John a large handful.

When they had left the shop John's mother asked him why he had not taken the cherries when the greengrocer had told him to.

"Well, you see Mummy," replied John, "his hand is twice as big as mine."

1 At what shop did John and his mother call first?
2 What was John doing while his mother was buying fruit?
3 What did the greengrocer tell John to do?
4 Did John do as he was told?
5 What did the greengrocer do when he saw John was so shy?
6 What did John's mother ask him after they had left the shop?
7 What was John's reply?

Write the missing words

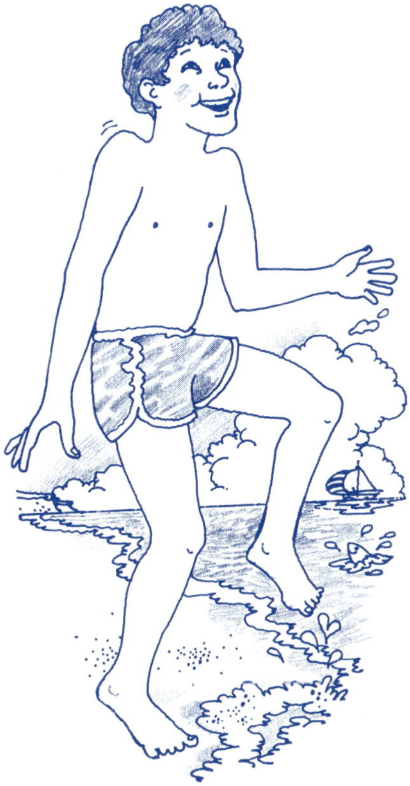

A

1 A sheep is covered with _____.
A rabbit is covered with _____.

2 A young cat is called a _____.
A young dog is called a _____.

3 A dog barks.
A lion _____.

4 The meat from a cow is called _____.
The meat from a pig is called _____.

5 A bus travels on land.
A ship travels on _____.

6 Mr. is a short way of writing Mister.
Dr. is a short way of writing _____.

7 You see with your eyes.
You smell with your _____.

8 Your foot is at the end of your _____.
Your hand is at the end of your _____.

B We can put these pairs of questions in a different way.

For the first pair we can write:

Sheep is to **wool** as **rabbit** is to _____.

The answer is **fur**, as you already know.

Now write the missing words.

1 **Cat** is to **kitten** as **dog** is to _____.

2 **Dog** is to **bark** as **lion** is to _____.

3 **Cow** is to **beef** as **pig** is to _____.

4 **Ship** is to **sea** as **bus** is to _____.

5 **Mr.** is to **Mister** as **Dr.** is to _____.

6 **See** is to **eyes** as **smell** is to _____.

Pictures and sentences

Write a sentence about each picture.
Some of the words are given to help you.

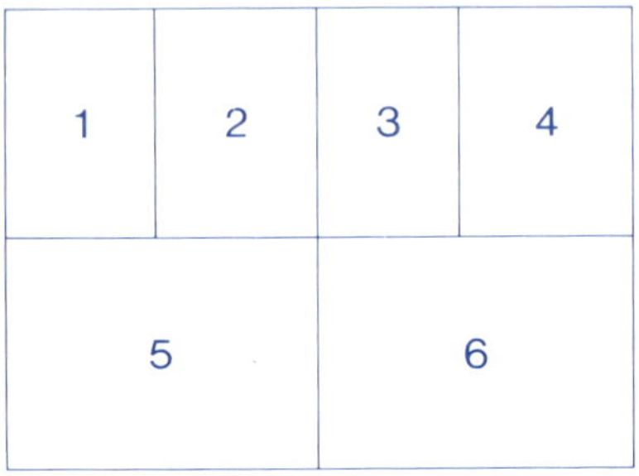

1 ____ man ____ cutting ____ tree ____ axe.

2 ____ giving ____ rabbit ____ leaf ____ lettuce.

3 ____ girl ____ watering ____ flowers ____ garden.

4 Ann ____ waiting ____ queue ____ bus stop.

5 Simon ____ sitting ____ river ____ catching ____ .

6 Peter ____ rowing ____ boat ____ towards ____ .

Telling the time

Look at the number to which the big hand points on each clock. Learn the times shown.

five minutes past

ten minutes past

twenty minutes past

twenty-five minutes past

five minutes to

ten minutes to

twenty minutes to

twenty-five minutes to

Each of these clocks shows the time a train leaves the station. Write the name of the place to which each train is going and the time of leaving.

1 The train to London leaves at . . . .

2 The Brighton train leaves at . . . .

3 The Edinburgh train leaves at . . . .

4 The train to Chester leaves at . . . .

5 The Birmingham train leaves at . . . .

6 The train to Torquay leaves at . . . .

7 The Bristol train leaves at . . . .

Using the right verb

bandage
catch
drive
fight
learn
plant
play
roast
row
strike

A Write the verb in the list on the left which fits each space.

1	to ____ a boat	6	to ____ a cold
2	to ____ meat	7	to ____ a game
3	to ____ a car	8	to ____ a battle
4	to ____ a tree	9	to ____ a cut
5	to ____ a lesson	10	to ____ a blow

built
mounted
packed
returned
sheltered
spent
stamped
taught
thanked
warmed

B Choose the right word from the list on the left to finish each sentence.

1 We ____ from the rain in an old barn.
2 James ____ from his holiday yesterday.
3 The carol singers ____ their feet to get warm.
4 Father ____ me to ride a bicycle.
5 Marion has ____ all her money.
6 I ____ the parcel and gave it to Michael.
7 Sally ____ herself by the blazing fire.
8 The new house was ____ in less than six months.
9 I ____ Susan for the lovely present she sent me.
10 The cowboy ____ his horse and rode off.

C Use each pair of words in a sentence of your own.

1	poked fire	4	burnt toast
2	sang carol	5	drank tea
3	posted letter	6	rang bell

Where they live

den
sty
web
nest
cage
hive
hutch
shell
kennel
stable

A Copy these sentences, filling each space with the name of the home of each creature. You can choose from the list of names on the left.

1 A snail carries its home, a _____, on its back.

2 The old sow and her piglets were lying down in their _____.

3 Martin made a cosy   for his pet rabbit.

4 The lion was in his _____ playing with his cubs.

5 Black Beauty was put in a _____ with another horse.

6 A swarm of bees flew out of the _____.

7 We watched the spider weaving its _____.

8 There are now two budgerigars in the _____.

9 The little terrier was fast asleep in his _____.

10 There were five eggs in the robin's _____.

B Arrange the words in each sentence in their right order. Begin each sentence with a capital letter, and end it with a full stop.

1 trees oak on grow Acorns

2 the from cow get We milk

3 a flower The spring is crocus

4 called a cow is from beef meat The

5 on River London the stands Thames

6 late train an was hour My

7 is called young kitten cat a A

8 warm Eskimos very clothes wear

Black Beauty and Ginger

My master and mistress made up their minds to pay a visit to some friends who lived about forty-six miles from our home. James was to drive them in the carriage, which was to be drawn by Ginger and me.

The first day we travelled thirty-two miles. There were some long, steep hills, but James drove so carefully that we were never tired or troubled. He never forgot to put on the brake as we went downhill, nor to take it off at the right place. He kept our feet on the smoothest part of the road; and if the uphill was very long he set the wheels a little across the road, so that the carriage should not run back, and gave us time to breathe. All these little things, together with kind words, help a horse very much.

We stopped once or twice on the road; and just as the sun was going down, we reached the town where we were to spend the night. We stopped at the biggest hotel, which was in the Market Place. We drove under an archway into a long yard, at the end of which were the stables where we were to rest.

Black Beauty Anna Sewell

1 What did Black Beauty's master and mistress make up their minds to do?
2 How far did they travel the first day?
3 Why were the horses never tired or troubled?
4 What did James do as they went downhill?
5 Why did James set the carriage wheels across the road when going up a long hill?
6 At what time of day did they reach the town?
7 Where did they stop?
8 Where were the stables in which the two horses were to spend the night?

Using ate and eaten

George **ate** his apple.

George **has eaten** his apple.

(**has** helps the word **eaten**)

The apple **was eaten** by George.

(**was** helps the word **eaten**)

The word **ate** needs no helping word.

The word **eaten** always has a helping word:

has eaten
have eaten
is eaten
are eaten
was eaten
were eaten
had eaten
and so on.

A Use **ate** or **eaten** to fill each space.

1 I ____
2 You have ____
3 It was ____
4 He ____
5 You ____
6 He has ____
7 We ____
8 They are ____
9 She ____
10 We had ____

B Fill each space with **ate** or **eaten**.

1 John ____ his supper and went to bed.
2 After John had ____ his supper he went to bed.
3 Many meals are ____ on the beach in summer.
4 The monkey ____ all the nuts the children gave him.
5 The jumper was ____ by moths.
6 The little bear's porridge had been ____ by Goldilocks.
7 The puppy ____ his food and looked for more.
8 When you have ____ your food you may leave the table.
9 Ian ____ the lean meat and left the fat.
10 Bread is ____ all over the world.

Rhymes

mouse
house
eyes
rise
day
way
hall
wall
quays
trees
noon
moon

The last word has been left out of each line in this poem. You will find these rhyming words in the list on the left.

A Copy the poem, filling in the missing words.

The moon

The moon has a face like the clock in the ____;
She shines on thieves on the garden ____,
On streets and fields and harbour ____,
And birdies asleep in the forks of ____.

The squalling cat and the squeaking ____,
The howling dog by the door of the ____,
The bat that lies in bed at ____,
All love to be out by the light of the ____.

But all of the things that belong to the ____
Cuddle to sleep to be out of her ____;
And flowers and children close their ____
Till up in the morning the sun shall ____.

B In each group below write three other words which rhyme with the word in bold type. The first letters are given to help you.

bat	2 **lard**	3 **tack**
r__ __	c__ __ __	r__ __ __
h__ __	y__ __ __	bl__ __ __
p__ __	h__ __ __	st__ __ __
and	5 **bag**	6 **lick**
h__ __ __	fl__ __	p__ __ __
br__ __ __	dr__ __	tr__ __ __
gr__ __ __	st__ __	qu__ __ __

Sentences

A Write the beginning of each sentence. Then choose the ending which will match it.

Example

1 The greedy boy was ill because he had eaten too much.

	Beginning	**Ending**
1	The greedy boy was ill	Simon looked hot and tired.
2	It was raining heavily	the ship of the desert.
3	As Robert was covered with spots	in a dozen.
4	After mowing the lawns	please let me know.
5	The camel is often called	and went off to school.
6	The load carried by a ship	that the ponds were frozen.
7	Paul picked up his satchel	because he had eaten too much.
8	If you want any help	his mother sent for the doctor.
9	The weather was so cold	is called a cargo.
10	There are twelve things	so Brian put on his mackintosh.

B Copy these beginnings. Add your own endings.

1 Roger burst into tears ....

2 Just as I left the house ....

3 Every Christmas Eve ....

4 While the cook was baking cakes ....

C Begin each sentence in your own way.

1 .... a very long way from home.

2 .... and we were soaking wet.

3 .... because he felt so tired.

4 .... so we could not travel by car.

Forming adjectives

Many adjectives are formed by adding **ful** to a noun.

Examples

hope+full=hope**ful**
(*full of hope*)

joy+full=joy**ful**
(*full of joy*)

Note that in adding **-full** one **l** is dropped.

beautiful	peaceful
careful	playful
harmful	thankful
helpful	truthful
painful	useful

A Choose from the list on the left the adjective ending with **-ful** which will fill each gap.

1	a kitten which is full of play	a ____ kitten
2	a village in which there is peace	a ____ village
3	a girl of great beauty	a ____ girl
4	a driver who takes great care	a ____ driver
5	a cut which gives much pain	a ____ cut
6	a book which is of great use	a ____ book
7	a friend who gives help	a ____ friend
8	a person who is full of thanks	a ____ person
9	a boy who speaks the truth	a ____ boy
10	a habit which causes harm	a ____ habit

B Add **-ful** to each of these words. Then choose three of the words you have made and use them in sentences of your own; one word in each sentence.

1 shame	3 wonder	5 hope
2 delight	4 cheer	6 hate

Opposites change of word

Learn the list of **opposites**, then answer the questions.

always	never
asleep	awake
better	worse
blunt	sharp
cruel	kind
evil	good
heavy	light
less	more
narrow	wide
pull	push

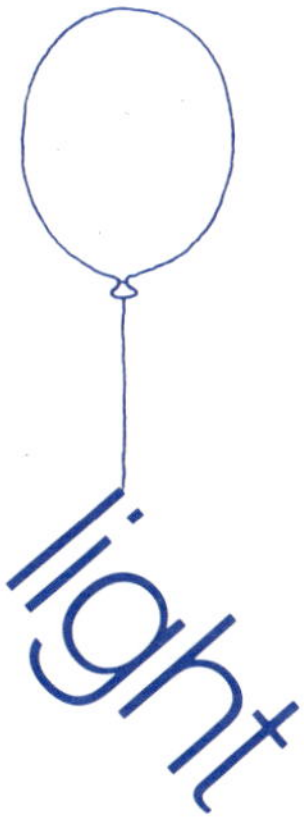

A Use the **opposite** of the word in bold type to fill each space.

Example a short story **long**

1 a ____ knife **sharp**

2 a ____ master **kind**

3 he was ____ **asleep**

4 ____ danger **more**

5 a ____ road **narrow**

6 a ____ parcel **light**

7 to ____ the door **push**

8 ____ tired **always**

9 a ____ player **better**

B Write the word which will fill each space.

1 You pull to open the door and ____ to close it.

2 The small box was quite ____ but the big one was heavy.

3 She could tell by his ____ smile that he was not a good man.

4 At seven o'clock Pat was wide awake, but Judith was still ____ .

5 The knife was blunt but the butcher soon made it ____ .

6 He always makes promises but ____ keeps them.

7 The road was wide in most places, but quite ____ in some.

8 Mary's cold was better this morning but it is ____ tonight.

9 The men wanted more pay and ____ work.

The end of the race

Amyntas drove himself forward in one last agonizing burst of speed, he was breathing against knives and the roar of the blood in his ears drowned the roar of the crowd. He was level with Leon – and then there was nothing ahead of him but the winning post.

The onlookers had crowded right down towards it; even above the howl of the blood in his head he heard them now, roar on solid roar of sound, shouting him in to victory. And then Hippias had caught him as he plunged past the post; and he was bending over the trainer's arm, bending over the pain in his belly, snatching at his breath and trying not to be sick. People were throwing sprigs of myrtle, he felt them flicking and falling on his head and shoulders. The sickness eased a little and his head was clearing; he began to hear friendly voices congratulating him, and Eudorus came shouldering through the crowd with a coloured ribbon to tie round his head.

The Truce of the Games Rosemary Sutcliff

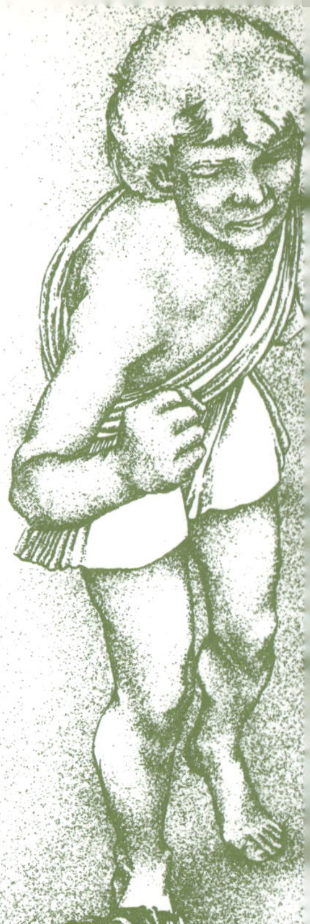

1 Which two competitors were leading in the race?
2 Explain what you think is meant by "breathing against knives".
3 Which two noises could Amyntas hear as he ran?
4 Write the words that tell you that the crowd hoped Amyntas would win.
5 What was the name of Amyntas' trainer?
6 What three discomforts did Amyntas suffer at the end?
7 What could he hear when his head began to clear?
8 What did he receive as a token of his victory?

Same sound — different meaning

Some words have the same sound as other words, but they differ in spelling and meaning.

Look at these four pairs of words.
Learn to spell each word.
Learn the meaning of each.

pain	He felt no **pain** when he had his tooth out.
pane	A new **pane** of glass was fixed in the window.
road	Many cars were parked at the side of the **road**.
rode	Ian **rode** to school on his new bicycle.
sail	One **sail** of the ship was torn by the strong wind.
sale	All goods were very cheap at the **sale**.
there	I left the dish **there**. (*in that place*)
their	The two boys had lost **their** pencils. (*belonging to them*)

Choose the correct word from the pair above to complete each sentence.

1 **road** **rode**
The ____ was muddy after the heavy rain.

2 **sail** **sale**
Helen bought the carpet at a ____ .

3 **pain** **pane**
Susan had a ____ in her arm.

4 **road** **rode**
Alan ____ his pony over the fields.

5 **there** **their**
We waited ____ for an hour.

6 **pain** **pane**
The cricket ball broke a ____ in the window.

7 **sail** **sale**
The ____ of the yacht was lowered as it reached the shore.

Containers

A **purse** holds or contains **money**.

A **jug** contains **water**.

Both are called **containers**.

bin
jug
vase
cup
purse
suitcase
basket
teapot
envelope

A Write the names of these containers. Look at the list on the left.

B Copy the sentences. Write the name of a container in each space.

1 Marion had no loose change in her ____ .

2 The ____ was full of rubbish.

3 I drink a ____ of tea at eleven o'clock every morning.

4 There was no milk left in the ____ .

5 Pack your clothes in this ____ .

6 Many people carry their shopping in a ____ .

7 David put the letter in the ____ and posted it.

8 There were some beautiful tulips in the ____ .

Using longer words

The word **where** can be joined to **any**, **every**, **no** and **some**.

any+where=**anywhere**

every+where=**everywhere**

no+where=**nowhere**

some+where=**somewhere**

A Use one of these longer words to fill each space.

1 The hammer must be ____ in the house.

2 We looked ____ for the lost hammer.

3 The hammer was ____ to be seen.

4 We could not find the hammer ____.

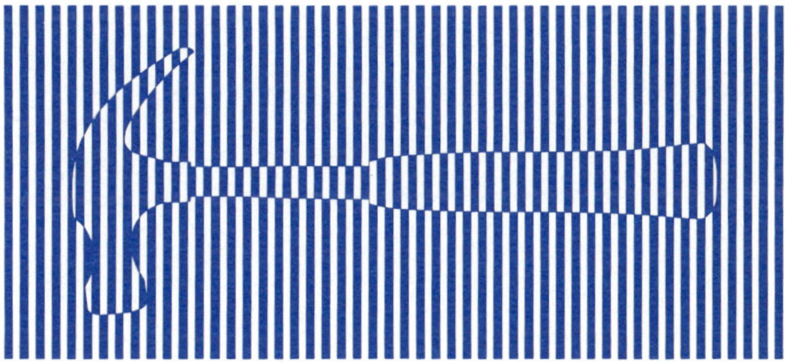

The word **body** can be joined to **any**, **every**, **no** and **some**.

any+body=**anybody**

every+body=**everybody**

no+body=**nobody**

some+body=**somebody**

B Write the words which will fill the gaps.

1 I don't think there is ____ at home.

2 We should be kind to ____.

3 You must get ____ to help you in the garden.

4 Jill knocked at the door but ____ answered.

The word **ever** can be joined to **when**, **where**, **who**, **what**, **how** and **which**.

whenever
wherever
whoever
whatever
however
whichever

C Write the **-ever** words which will finish these sentences.

1 He never wears a hat ____ cold the weather is.

2 People must buy food ____ it costs.

3 ____ took the money must give it back.

4 You can visit us ____ you like.

Joining sentences using because

The word **because** can be used to join two sentences.

Example

The dog bit John.
He was teasing it.

two sentences

The dog bit John **because** he was teasing it.

one sentence

A Use **because** to join these sentences.

1 Roy was very happy.
There was a holiday.

2 He did not drink his tea.
It was cold.

B Use **and** to join these sentences.

1 Peter dropped the cup.
It broke.

2 Henry went into the park.
He had a ride on the swing.

C Use **but** to join these sentences.

1 It was a lovely hat.
It was too small for Penny.

2 We waited for Carol.
She did not turn up.

D Use **so** to join these sentences.

1 The weather was bitterly cold.
Colin wore gloves.

2 Robin was a naughty boy.
He was sent to bed early.

E Write the missing word **and**, **but**, **so**, **because** in each sentence.

1 We were thirsty ____ we called at a farm for a glass of milk.

2 Michael wanted to swim ____ his mother said it was too cold.

3 Barbara made the cakes ____ put them in the oven.

4 He felt cold ____ he had no overcoat.

Words with more than one meaning

Some words have more than one meaning.

We went to visit an old tin **mine** in Cornwall.

The red towel is **mine** but the blue one belongs to Sally.

blind
felt
foot
long
mean
ring
rock
suit
top
trunk

Use the words in the list on the left to fill these spaces. The same word must be used for each pair of sentences.

1 The dress is too _____ so I must shorten it.
I often _____ for a holiday in Spain.

2 The miser was too _____ to buy food for himself.
Some words _____ much the same as other words.

3 I think this dress will _____ you.
Henry wore a navy blue _____ at the wedding.

4 Under the carpet was a layer of _____.
Carol _____ ill, so she went to bed early.

5 A _____ person cannot see.
She pulled the _____ down over the window.

6 Mother packed the _____ for the holidays.
The elephant took the bun with his long _____.

7 There was a hostel at the _____ of the mountain.
He was lame because he had hurt his _____.

8 Please _____ the doorbell.
Emma wore a _____ on each finger.

9 On the beach was a huge _____.
Jane tried to _____ the baby to sleep.

10 Humpty Dumpty was sitting on _____ of the wall.
The red _____ was spinning round and round.

A bear cub's adventure

Bears have an excellent sense of smell, and very keen hearing; . . . and scent the faintest odour from a great distance. This is fortunate for them, as they are very short-sighted.

A breeze arose, wafting the odour of something sweet towards Mishook the bear cub. What could it be? The cub did not know, but his mother and the elder ones recognised the aroma of honey . . .

With hurried steps the whole bear family set off in search of the prize. They trotted along for about a kilometre before they reached the old decayed tree-trunk where the bees had taken up their abode. The poor bees saw the plunderers, and immediately sounded an alarm. They then defended their store of honey . . . by fiercely stinging the bears.

But the mother bear and her cubs . . . calmly continued their feast of honey, their thick fur protecting them against the attacks of the bees. One angry bee, however, plunged its sting into Mishook's nose. He growled furiously, shook his head, jumped, snorted, turned round like a spinning-top, and it was with great difficulty that he managed to beat off the troublesome insect with his paws. But this repulse did not by any means prevent him from tasting his share of the honey, of which he immediately became very fond.

Baby Mishook Leon Golschmann

1. Bears have two senses which are more well-developed than the others. What are they?
2. Why are the bears fortunate in having these senses?
3. What was the odour which the breeze blew towards Mishook?
4. Where had the bees taken up their abode?
5. What did the bees do when they saw the bears approaching?
6. How did the bees defend their store of honey?
7. Why were the bears able to continue their feast of honey?
8. Which of the bear family was stung by an angry bee?
9. Describe how this bear got rid of the troublesome insect.

Writing sentences about pictures

Write one sentence about what each person is doing in this picture. The words in the list will help you.

cutting
field
filling
flying
garden
hanging
hedge
kite
lawn
line
mowing
outside
painting
tap
washing
water
watering can

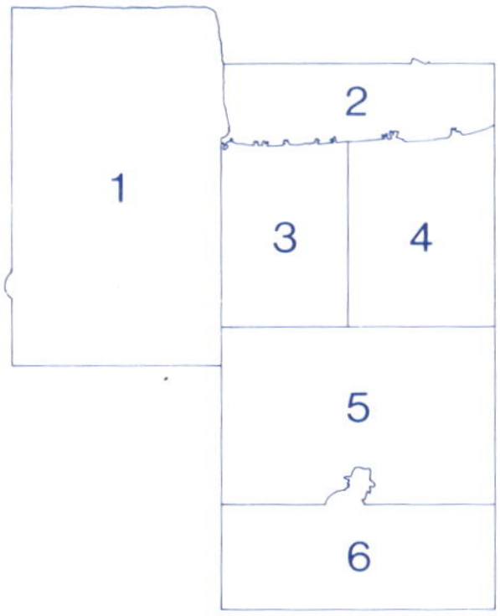

Using gave and given

Aunt Judy **gave** Paul fifty pence.

Aunt Judy **has given** Paul fifty pence.

(**has** helps the word **given**)

Paul **was given** fifty pence by Aunt Judy.

(**was** helps the word **given**)

The word **gave** needs no helping word.

The word **given** always has a helping word:

has given
have given
is given
are given
was given
were given
had given
and so on.

A Use **gave** or **given** to fill each space.

1	He has ____	6	We have ____
2	She ____	7	I ____
3	It was ____	8	They have ____
4	You ____	9	They were ____
5	They had ____	10	We ____

B Write the word which fills each space.

1 The teacher ____ each child a new pencil.

2 Each child was ____ a new pencil.

3 All the pens were ____ out.

4 Ann has ____ Carol a sweet.

5 Terry ____ me a big red apple.

6 Jennifer ____ her parents a kiss before going to bed.

7 Every child at the party will be ____ a toy.

8 Mary was sorry that she had ____ all her sweets away.

9 Colin liked the bat which Uncle Fred ____ him.

Things which are alike

When something is very light in weight we say it is as **light** as a **feather**.

This is because a feather is so very, very light.

Learn the sayings in the list below.

as black as pitch
as brown as a berry
as easy as A B C
as green as grass
as hard as nails
as hot as fire
as soft as putty
as sour as vinegar
as stiff as a poker
as weak as a kitten

A Write the missing words.

1 as weak as a ____
2 as sour as ____
3 as easy as ____
4 as brown as a ____
5 as green as ____
6 as hard as ____
7 as stiff as a ____
8 as soft as ____
9 as black as ____

B

1 as ____ as fire
2 as ____ as grass
3 as ____ as nails
4 as ____ as a kitten
5 as ____ as a poker
6 as ____ as vinegar
7 as ____ as pitch
8 as ____ as a berry

C Write the missing words.

1 John felt as weak as a ____ after his illness.
2 The soldier held himself as stiff as a ____.
3 He returned from the seaside as brown as a ____.
4 The cooking apple was as ____ as vinegar.
5 Andrew found the sum as easy as ____.

Sounds

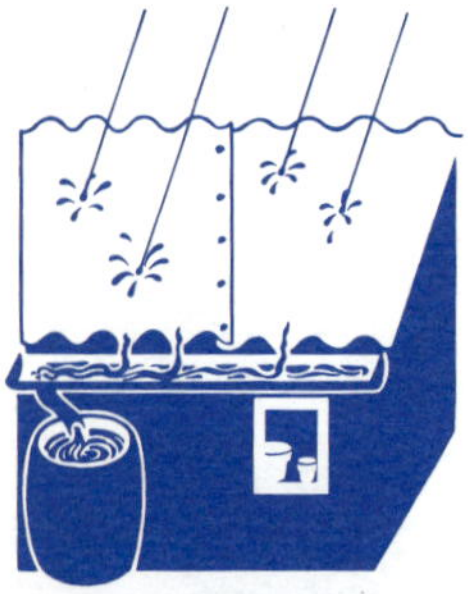

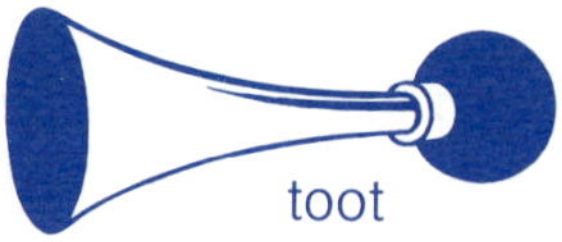

A Write the name of each sound.

1 the ____ of dishes

2 the ____ of a drum

3 the ____ of bells

4 the ____ of a clock

5 the ____ of a door

6 the ____ of a horn

7 the ____ of a kettle

8 the ____ of raindrops

B Write the **sound** word which suits each sentence.

1 The ____ of raindrops on the window awakened the children.

2 We heard the ____ of drums as the soldiers drew near.

3 The room was so quiet that we could hear the ____ of the clock.

4 The ____ of the kettle told us that tea was nearly ready.

5 From the kitchen came the ____ of dishes.

6 With a ____ of the door Brian left the room in a bad temper.

7 The car went past with a ____ of the horn.

8 Every Sunday the ____ of church bells could be heard in the village.